Memories of
MAIN STREET

Carney Mill stretched from North Main Street to the current Medical Park Drive.

Memories of
MAIN STREET

*Atmore, Alabama — A Special Place
Remembered in Words and Pictures*

Nancy Bosenberg Karrick

NewSouth

Montgomery

TNSB
NewSouth, Inc.
105 S. Court Street
Montgomery, AL 36104

Copyright © 2023 by Nancy Bosenberg Karrick.
All rights reserved under International and Pan-American Copyright Conventions.

ISBN 978-1-961938-00-7

Printed in the United States of America

This history of the buildings and businesses in downtown Atmore, Alabama, is dedicated to the memory of the ones who gave me the opportunity to grow up in C. K. Carter General Merchandise on Main Street:

My grandparents, Comer and Nancy Carter,

My aunt and uncle, Mildred and Bill Dunaway,

And my parents, Charles and Velma Bosenberg;

And also to the memory of my husband and research partner, Charles Karrick.

— Nancy Bosenberg Karrick

Table of Street Addresses

Address	Page
204 South Main Street	17
101 West Church Street	18
132 South Main Street	21
128–130 South Main Street	22
130 South Main Street	23
122 South Main Street	24
120 South Main Street	27
116 South Main Street	29
114 and 112 South Main Street	31
108 South Main Street	33
102 and 100 South Main Street	37
107 (109) West Nashville Avenue	39
111 West Nashville Avenue	40
100 South Trammell Street	41
101 North Trammell Street	42
100 North Trammell Street	43
110 West Louisville Avenue	44
108 West Louisville Avenue	47
104–102 West Louisville Avenue	48
100 West Louisville Avenue	49
101–103 North Main Street	50
105 North Main Street	52
109 North Main Street	54
111 North Main Street	55
113 North Main Street	56
115 North Main Street	56
117 North Main Street	58
119 North Main Street	59
121 North Main Street	60
123 North Main Street	61
125 North Main Street	62
127–129 North Main Street	62
131–133 North Main Street	63
135 North Main Street	64
137 North Main Street	65
201 North Main Street, 100 West Ridgeley	70
102 West Ridgeley Street	70
104 West Ridgeley Street	71
106 West Ridgeley Street	71
108 West Ridgeley Street	72
110 West Ridgeley Street	72
112 West Ridgeley Street	73
114 West Ridgeley Street	75
116 West Ridgeley Street	75
111 West Ridgeley Street	76
109 West Ridgeley Street	76
107 West Ridgeley Street	77
105 West Ridgeley Street	77
201 North Main Street	78
205 North Main Street	79
207 North Main Street	80
206 North Main Street	81
204–202 North Main Street	82
200 North Main Street	83
126 North Main Street	84
124 North Main Street	84
122 North Main Street	86
114 North Main Street	87
112–110 North Main Street	88
108 North Main Street	89
104 North Main Street	90
102–100 North Main Street	90
101 East Louisville Avenue	92
103 East Nashville Avenue	92
105 East Louisville Avenue	93
107 East Louisville	94
102 East Nashville Avenue	97
104 East Nashville Avenue	97
106 East Nashville Avenue	98
108 East Nashville Avenue	99
110 East Nashville Avenue	99
114–112 East Nashville Avenue	100
118 East Nashville Avenue	101
120 East Nashville Avenue	102
122 East Nashville Avenue	103
200 East Nashville Avenue	104
101 South Main Street	106
111 South Main Street	107
119 South Main Street	109
121 South Main Street	110
125 South Main Street	111
129 South Main Street	112
201 South Main Street	113
205 South Main Street	113

Contents

Table of Street Addresses / vi

Preface / ix

Glossary / xii

Introduction / 3

The Streetscapes / 5

The Buildings / 17

The Memories / 115

Bibliography and Notes / 145

About the Author / 149

Index / 150

Closing Photos / 160

Atmore's Main Street, about 1912, from the south.

Preface

In November 1987, while living in Belgium where my husband, Charles Karrick, was stationed with the U.S. Army, we made a trip to England. One of the places I wanted to visit was the site of the origin of the nursery rhyme, "Ride a Cock Horse to Banbury Cross." When we arrived in Banbury, what we saw was a feast for our eyes. This city, which had been around since before the thirteenth century, was full of beautiful, ancient buildings. Even more exciting was a bookstore which had a book for sale titled *Memories of Banbury*. Not only did I purchase the book, but the author was on site and autographed it. This delightful book gave memories of the town through pictures and words. It was a tremendous help to us as it explained the history of the buildings while we walked along the sidewalks on our way to the famous cross. It struck my mind that this type of book would be a wonderful project for downtown Atmore.

Fast forward about ten years and a move back to my hometown of Atmore, Alabama. Keeping my Banbury book in mind, I started asking older citizens of Atmore to tell me their memories of the town when they were in school. What I heard excited me, because I realized that Atmore was really an up-and-coming place to live in the 1930s through the 1960s. Looking back in time, I realized that the town was alive and active while I was growing up in the last of Atmore's glory days, when downtown was *the* place to be.

In 1997, I took a series of pictures of downtown Atmore buildings and put them into a scrapbook. With scrapbook in hand, I went to even more elder citizens, showed them the pictures, and asked what they knew about the buildings and the businesses located in them. My story was developing, but I still had big gaps in the history.

It was about this time that Charles was working on a book on the history of the Bank of Atmore and was planning a research trip to the Alabama Department of Archives and History in Montgomery. I went along with

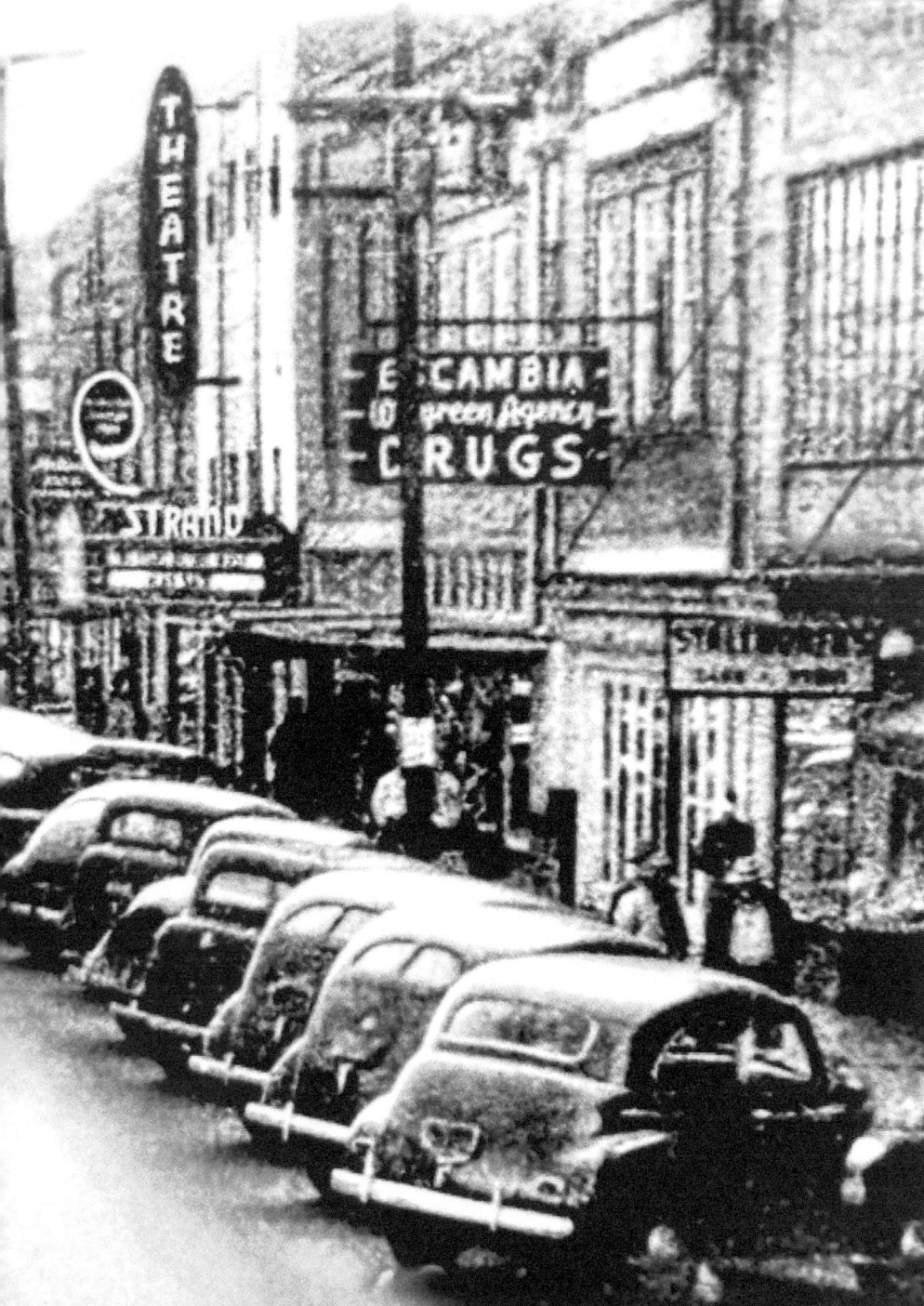

Bustling South Main Street, 1930s.

him and looked for information on businesses in Atmore, using microfiche of old issues of the *Atmore Record* and the *Atmore Spectrum* newspapers. Charles made several more trips to Montgomery to gather information for his book. When I couldn't accompany him because I was at work, he would copy articles and ads for me concerning downtown Atmore. His research was valuable to both of our endeavors. We did many joint interviews with people who had knowledge of the bank and had lived in Atmore for many years. The two book subjects were so connected that it was easy to combine our efforts.

It took retirement for me, and also Covid 19 quarantine, to pick up the project again and finish it. Time, I now had plenty of. I had pages of handwritten interview notes. I had lots of ideas about what downtown was like in Atmore's early years. What I didn't have was most of the people I had interviewed earlier or people who were in Atmore in the early 1910s. I realized that time was taking its toll, and if I wanted to get this information safely recorded, I needed to get it finished.

One of my largest obstacles was the absence of my grandparents and parents. They were a part of downtown Atmore from 1919 on and could have told me so much if I had just asked. I realized I was having to rely on my memories for many things because I was the only one in my family left who spent a large amount of time in a store on Main Street.

I feel I need to make some disclaimers. I interviewed many older people for this book. The information they gave me may or may not be accurate, but it was their memories. Secondly, many buildings underwent physical changes over the decades, and it was sometimes hard for people to be sure exactly which building a particular business occupied. Third, several commercial buildings were divided into two or more separate stores, or, in some cases, separate stores were combined to form a larger building. Because of this, street addresses often skip numbers or are out of order. Working this out was like assembling a large jigsaw puzzle of downtown Atmore into a complete picture.

I HOPE THAT READERS will use this volume as I used my Banbury book—as a guidebook with information of who and what was in these local buildings many years ago.

To take advantage of the book, begin at the American Legion Building and stroll along the sidewalk on the southwest side of Main Street, continue along west Nashville, cross the railroad tracks, go along west Louisville, turn back on Main Street, go left at Ridgeley, and circle back to Main and proceed north. You will need to cross Main either at Main and Ridgeley or about a half block north.

Headed down the east side of Main, take a left on east Louisville and come back to the Main Street railroad crossing to get to east Nashville. Walk toward United Bank, taking advantage of one of the benches along the way for a rest. With luck, you might even get to watch a train come rolling through town.

Retrace your steps back to Main Street and turn left. Proceed two blocks and you will have completed the downtown tour. If you're thirsty, there is a good place to get something to drink right across the street. Sit for a while, thumb through your book, and recall some of your own memories of the downtown area in our special town of Atmore.

Glossary

BALUSTER A short pillar or column, typically decorative in design, in a series supporting a rail or coping.

BAY Section of a building distinguished by vertical elements such as columns or pillars. Often protrudes from the surface of the wall in which it is situated, thus creating a small nook-like interior space.

BELT COURSE A continuous row or layer of stones or brick set in a wall. When set in a line with window sills, it helps to make the horizontal line of the sills visually more prominent. When set between the floors of a house, it helps to make the separate floors distinguishable from the exterior of the building.

BRACKET A projection from a vertical surface which provides structural and/or visual support for overhanging elements such as cornices, balconies, and eaves.

COPING The top course of a brick or stone wall.

CORBEL A projection jutting out from a wall to support a structure above it.

CORNICE Any horizontal decorative molding which crowns a building.

DOUBLE HUNG WINDOWS Window with top and bottom sashes which slide past each other vertically. Allows ventilation from the top, bottom, or both parts of the window.

FACADE The face of a building, especially the front which looks onto a street or open space.

LINTEL A horizontal support of timber, stone, concrete, or steel across the top of a door or window.

MASONRY Being of stone, brick, or concrete.

MULLION A heavy vertical or horizontal bar between the panes of glass in a window.

MUNTIN Narrow strips of wood which divide the individual panes of glass in a traditional window.

PARAPET A low protective wall along the edge of a roof, bridge, or balcony.

PIER Massive vertical support of masonry, placed under columns, arches, or walls to support a concentration of loads.

PILASTER A rectangular column, especially one projecting from a wall. Resembles a square post attached to a wall.

SCUPPER An outlet in the side of a building for draining water.

SHED ROOF Type of roof with a single slope and rafters spanning from one wall to another.

TERRA COTTA Unglazed, typically brownish-red earthenware, used chiefly as an ornamental building material and in modeling.

TRANSOM A small window placed above a door or window.

Memories of
MAIN STREET

Introduction

It is hard to believe that the site of present-day Atmore was once a wet area containing ponds full of alligators and lily pads. Also present were pine trees, which became the lifeblood of the town through the lumber and turpentine industries.

The 1860s brought the railroad through the area all the way to the Tensaw River. There was no town here. It did, however, become a railroad stop with the name of Williams' Station. The name was after William Larkin Williams, who lived about ten miles down into Florida. The location was where the train would drop off supplies for Mr. Williams, thus the name Williams' Station.

By 1895, the town had grown to a population of 165. Many of the workers at the local sawmill lived out of town, so two hotels, the Magnolia and the Emmons, opened to offer them temporary quarters. According to an ad in the October 2, 1903, *Atmore Spectrum,* proprietor E. L. Pipkin had opened the third hotel, The Atmore. The ad mentions the establishment's stable, horses, buggies, and polite drivers, but says nothing about the rooms!

In 1895, the people in Williams' Station decided they needed a more appropriate name for their growing town. Atmore was eventually selected after Charles Pawson Atmore, the General Ticket Agent for the Louisville and Nashville Railroad.

Atmore grew in population, churches and schools were established, and the downtown began to develop. From the original Carney Store, which also included a post office, another early store was Roberts', on what is now east Nashville about where the standing clock is on the railroad side of First National Bank. Farther north was Tidmore and Ward's, on Ashley Street—the location of the famous Railroad Bill killing. W. W. Lowery had a store about where the Strand is on south Main Street. Atmore Hardware opened in 1898 at the intersection of Main and Church streets and moved to its better-known location on south Main in 1904.

While timber and turpentine gave Atmore its start, King Cotton took it to its glory days. Many of us remember the wagons and trucks cruising the streets, their drivers calling out for cotton pickers. The talk of the day was the price of cotton per pound and how many bales to the acre were being picked. The hottest contest every year was who would get the first bale of cotton ginned. Streets were lined with wisps of cotton, and window screens clogged with cotton lint. Gins were humming day and night. Wagons full of cotton lined the streets all over town as they waited to have their cotton ginned. Life was good—hard, but good—and the economy prospered. As it prospered, downtown grew, and with that growth came more events and activities for citizens to enjoy.

Atmore, which is located in southwest Alabama about fifty miles north of both Mobile and Pensacola, had a population in 2022 of approximately ten thousand. Downtown is compact enough that it can be completely covered and explored by foot.

In addition to viewing the downtown area, visitors and residents alike should take time to look at the old Williams' Station Cemetery, located at the west end of Church Street, just to the side of the railroad trestle. There, you will see many graves of some of our earliest citizens. Tour leaflets for the cemetery are available at the Atmore Welcome Center in Heritage Park on South Main Street or the Atmore Chamber of Commerce at 137 North Main Street.

The Streetscapes

Northwest side of Main Street, 2017.

200 block of Southeast Main Street, 2017.

Corner of South Main and Church streets, 1997.

Northwest Main Street, looking south, early 2000s.

The Streetscapes

Southwest Main Street, early 2000s.

Northwest Ridgeley Street before renovation, 1997.

Northwest Ridgeley Street, 2000s.

East Main Street, looking north.

The Streetscapes

West Main Street, looking south.

Memories of Main Street

East Nashville Avenue. The bottom photo is from a different vantage, but continues from the right of the top photo.

The Buildings

204 South Main Street
ATMORE HARDWARE

The location of the old Atmore Hardware warehouse is empty except for its bare concrete floor. Hurricane damage, plus the fact that the Atmore Hardware business closed in 1994, made it not feasible to repair the large storage building used by the hardware store. The concrete slab, now replaced by a park, was just south of the current American Legion building.

Robert Maxwell noted that James Wearren and Pellar Webb made trips to the warehouse when something was sold at the hardware store. His brother Ben, who later became Dr. Ben Maxwell, worked there in high school.

Haskew Middleton remembered that it looked like a horse barn for years and was used to store roofing and building materials. Before the slab was poured, the floor was dirt.

The building was a two-story metal warehouse with front oriented gables. There were twenty-two metal fixed windows throughout and a poured concrete foundation.

Park at site of former Atmore Hardware warehouse.

101 West Church Street
AMERICAN LEGION, LIBRARY, CARNEY LODGE

For years, the door to the Legion Building was facing the corner of Main and Church streets. That door was eventually relocated to the Church Street side of the building, which gave access to other businesses located in the structure. There is also a side entrance which opened up to the old Atmore Public Library.

The Atmore Public Library, which was first located in the upstairs of the old Bank of Atmore building on North Main Street, was moved to the Carney Lodge, Number 549, and the Atmore Record Building located on the corner of South Main Street and West Church Street, which is the present site of the American Legion Building. When the Carney Lodge Building, a wooden structure, was torn down in 1945 to make room for the new brick Legion Building, the library was moved to the council room of the old Atmore City Hall. When the Legion Building was completed in 1949, rooms were leased by the Atmore City Council to house the Atmore Public Library. Mrs. Jane Peavy was appointed librarian. The library left the Legion Building in 1963 to move into a new building on South Trammell Street.

In 1944, plans were put in place for erection of a modern brick and steel structure to be known as "Legion Memorial Building" in honor of World War II servicemen and women. Post World War II, Legion membership was over 550, and a new

The American Legion Building at Main and Church. Its cornerstone reads:

IN HONOR OF OUR MEN AND WOMEN
WHO SERVED IN DEFENSE OF THEIR
COUNTRY WW ONE AND TWO 1917–1918,
1941–1945.
AMERICAN LEGION POST #90. DEDICATED
NOVEMBER 11, 1949
T. M. HAND COMMANDER 1948
W. K. MCCONNICO 1949
W. R. MAXWELL, JR. ADJUTANT
J. B. SWIFT, SR. BUILDING CHAIRMAN

and larger facility was needed. The present American Legion Building was built on Masonic property with a ninety-nine-year lease. In 2005, the post purchased the property from the Masons for $35,000, owning the land and building free and clear.[1]

Many of Atmore's citizens had fond memories of the "Legion Hall," as the building was best known. Velma Bosenberg grew up as a child going to the library in the old wooden Legion Building. Haskew Middleton, a fifty-year member of the American Legion, recounted that Byard Swift, Chester Benton, and Johnny Jones were instrumental in raising money to build the building. Beer and slot machines were often used to add to the money coffers. Usage of those slot machines also had a strange story. I loved the story the Legionnaires told about the slots. Before he came to raid the building, the sheriff would notify the Legion so that they could get out of the building, usually by the fire escape. Bill Ward, the local ABC man, would send word when the state people were coming. This gave the men ample time to avoid being caught.

Lukie and Mirtis Anderson remembered when the jail was located where the old Faircloth's Grocery was, just to the side and behind the Legion Building. Robert Maxwell also remembered the jail as being directly behind the Legion on Church Street. It was a two-story masonry building with bars on the windows. During World War II, lard and other hog renderings were used for explosives which were made in Sylacauga. The first floor of the jail served as a storage place for Atmore Boys Lard Collection. The lard was heated, then hardened, and brought to the jail for storage before being shipped to Sylacauga. He said the building ceased to be a jail in the early 1940s. Robert also recalled Miss Elsie Schott as the librarian where he first learned to be quiet in a library. John Webb commented that Miss Schott's father was a Baptist preacher.

Joel Day said that in the 1980s Haywood Harper had a band in Bay Minette and asked Joel if there was a place in Atmore to have dances with no bar. Commander Stanton said the band could use the second floor of the Legion Building if they would fix it up from storm damage. Leonard Stanley and Joel and Louise Day worked to clean the room up. Harper came and started Saturday dances. Money collected was used for new tables and chairs. Day also remembered that the second floor was used for gospel music and square dances. After Hurricane Ivan tore up the upper floors on September 16, 2004, the dances were moved downstairs.

Helaine Birnberg recalled that in the days before the current Legion Building was constructed, dances were held in the old wooden American Legion. One or two parents would have the dance where the only entertainment was a Victrola. Punch was served, and it was really something to get a new dress to wear.

In her book *Grace Was in Their Steps*, former Atmore resident Marcia Webb Pepperman noted that Atmore Hardware was first located at the Legion Building location before it moved up the street in 1904.

In addition to housing the American Legion and the Atmore Public Library, the building or site has also been home over the years to Atmore Hardware, U.S. Navy Recruiting Station, Linda's Hair Fashions, Jack's Barber Shop, Eleanor's House of Beauty, Taylor Faircloth's fabric store, Masonic Hall, City Furniture, Atmore Rug and Shade, Coleman's Singer Sewing Machines, Mrs. Gidden's Beauty Shop, Pappy Taylor's Barber Shop, Booker Barber Shop, OK Barber Shop, City Furniture, Kevin McKinley's law office, Gayle's Income Tax and Hall's Income Tax. There were probably others I'm not aware of.

The structure is a three-story brick building with Art Deco influences and a flat roof. Fixed metal windows are on the first floor and double hung windows on second and third floor. There is an entrance bay only attached porch with a two-story wing. The rounded front entrance on the corner of the building with a round metal awning has been closed off, and an entrance on Church Street serves as the main entrance.

The first time this author can remember going into the American Legion building was in the mid 1950s when I entered the side door with my aunt and walked into a wonderland of books. During the summer months, I walked through that door every day that the library was open and usually walked out with the maximum number of books allowed. Books, not television, were my passion, and with the help of Mrs. Jane Peavy, the librarian, I traveled to many exotic places and solved many of Nancy Drew's mysteries. As I grew older, I watched my uncle, Bill Dunaway, put on his American Legion cap and go to meetings, and later my husband, Charles Karrick, became Commander of Post 90. I am an American Legion Auxiliary member. I reckon that old building has been a part of my life almost from the start.[2]

This monument at 204 S. Main was moved in 2022 from the Church Street side.

From cars to gowns to flowers . . . all have been here.

132 South Main Street
GREATER FAIR, THE FORGET-ME-NOT

From greasy cars to elegant gowns, this building has housed it all. Almost every person interviewed mentioned Lamont and Sowell Garage, the Forget-Me-Not, and Greater Fair. Charles and Velma Bosenberg sang high praises to the Greater Fair, run by Agnes Smith. Not only did they have lovely clothes, but the service was par excellence.

When the author was living overseas with her military husband, Agnes Smith would let Mother send me boxes of clothes with the option to return them if they did not fit or I did not like them. I remember very few being returned. The only exception was when I was sent four evening dresses for an event I only needed one for. Three had to be returned, but I wore the one I kept for several years. Since American style clothes were hard to find in Europe at the time, the service offered by Agnes Smith was greatly appreciated.

John Webb mentioned that Willie Lamont and Charlie Sowell had a garage with gas tanks out front and did service work. Mr. Sowell was the father of Catherine and Margaret Sowell. Robert Maxwell said they had a large door opening so it was possible to drive through the garage. Lukie Anderson said that Bobby Davis's mother was the bookkeeper. Mr. Sowell and L. E. Dickinson had a furniture store which eventually evolved into Dickinson Furniture. In the late 1940s or early '50s, Dickinson and Henry Barnett opened as Dickinson and Barnett Furniture. In 1952, when Dickinson moved to Church Street, he gave the American Legion couches, chairs, a television and lamps at cost, according to Haskew Middleton. James Forte elaborated on the front of the building, saying it was cut off at an angle with gas pumps under an awning. Dickinson and Henry Barnett bought the building and squared the front as it is today.

Elise Crook said that Frances Solomon, from

Greenville, started the Forget-Me-Not Shop. The Greater Fair opened in 1930, next to the pool room on East Nashville Avenue. When the Forget-Me-Not closed, Agnes Smith moved her store to the Main Street location it enjoyed until 1988. It became "*The* Store in Atmore—Offering the Finest in Fashions, Especially for Women," as noted in its advertising. Men were taken care of at Henley's Men's Shoppe, a project of Henley Smith, Agnes's husband. Just before closing for good, the store was downsized and named Simply Agnes. Vera Lufkin said, "I was amazed at the selection of clothes at the Greater Fair. Some were pricey and I would wait until they were marked down and then get them. Agnes had good taste." Most of the ladies and girls in town would agree that the clothes from the Greater Fair were as stylish as any in the larger cities' stores, with the convenience of buying in Atmore.

The building has also been home to the Beans Store where healthy foods and gifts were sold, Movie Time Video and Arcade, and now is home to Atmore Flower Shop.

The structure is one story with a flat roof and a limestone cap. It has a recessed entrance, flanked by display windows. A recessed sign panel runs the width of the building, and below that is a series of four evenly placed and slightly recessed windows, each with fixed wood and ten panes. It has aluminum and glass doors.

128–130 South Main Street
ATMORE NEWS

The *Atmore News* was started at 128 South Main Street in June 2005 by Sherry Digmon, Myrna Monroe, and Ryan Carter, joining with Grace Publishing and *atmore Magazine*. The building has been the home of numerous businesses since its construction in the early to mid twenties. Lukie and Mirtis Anderson, James Forte, Cliff Frazier, Byard Swift, and Jack Lufkin remembered Charlie Steele having Steele's Cash and Carry at that location. Mattie Lou Crook said Charlie Steele gave her a job there, with the only work she did being at the cash register and stacking snuff and baby food. Robert Maxwell and Lowell McGill said Melvin Nall also had a grocery store in that location.

Vera Lufkin, Bill Chapman, Ellie Bailey, and Mattie Lou Crook recalled Wingard's on Main. Mattie Lou said that Brent Whittaker owned the building and Mary

Wingard rented and spent a lot of money remodeling it. The building was actually divided into two parts, with Wise Insurance also having a location there as well as Skipper Insurance Company. Wingard's closed in 1996 after 43 years in business.

Other occupants were New York Life with Gwen Dorriety and Nancy Lowrey, Financial Solutions with Greg Dorriety, Merle Norman Beauty Center run by Bernece Presley, and a dispatch center for Crimson Trucking Company.

This building appears to have been built at the same time as the one on the north side, either as a single building or purposefully divided in half as the exteriors are identical. The structure is one story with a parapet flat roof with simple decorative brick cornices. It is made of brick with a continuous foundation. Decorative vent holes in the shape of a flat diamond are above each bay. This side of the building is covered with wood siding and has tall rectangular windows on the front with a recessed entrance. While this side of the building is numbered 128, its twin to the north is 130. Numerically, those numbers should be switched to follow correct numbering order.

130 South Main Street
THE TOT SHOP

The physical description for the Tot Shop building numbered 130 South Main is the same as just given for 128 South Main. The major difference is the aluminum and glass door and storefront windows which were installed in the 1960s, probably about the time the store moved from North Main to its current location. Its construction date is listed as 1925, but it may actually be older than that date.

Mary B. Anderson, usually called Snookie, opened the Tot Shop in 1948 on East Nashville Avenue. It soon moved to a larger space at 107 North Main and in 1964 moved to its present location at 130 South Main Street. Son Carl runs the store now.

My mother would drive all the way from Pensacola

Opposite page, the Atmore News, and left, the Tot Shop, which share a building on South Main.

just to come to "Snookie's" to buy my clothes. You would think that with the selection of stores in Pensacola she would have shopped there. That's not to say she didn't ever shop in Pensacola because she did. She also made most of my clothes, but it was always back to Atmore we would come when she wanted something really special, different, and well-made. The Tot Shop filled the bill nicely. Besides, she and Snookie could chat and visit.³ Velma Bosenberg and I made the trip to The Tot Shop many times over the years and always came away satisfied with our purchases.

Before The Tot Shop occupied the building, it was home to the A&P grocery store. Mr. Malone managed the store, and Robert Maxwell worked as a clerk. He said that he got off at 8 on Saturday night and at 11:30 when he worked for Cliff Bethea. People came by after the late movie for groceries. Drunetta Hammack recalled fond memories of trips to the A&P. According to the 1964 Polk's directory, a shoe shop was at the location. Haskew Middleton said Pee Wee Bethea's wife had a shoe store but did not remember the name. Harper Dry Goods was on the right side at one time and a beauty shop which Gwen Dorriety's sister owned and Paula Daniels worked at was also at this location.

122 South Main Street

SWEET SHOP, CRAWFORD'S CAFE, POST OFFICE, DRY GOODS

Back in 1885, W. M. Carney owned the property where the Sweet Shop was eventually located. In 1889, W. W. Lowery built a brick building and a house there. By the 1910 census, a two-story building, which was part commercial, was noted. The post office became a tenant in

The Sweet Shop.

1913 and remained there until 1923. In 1930, the building was sold to Rankin Lowery who later sold it to C. B. Crawford. The Crawfords lived on the second floor and ran Crawford's Cafe on the first. Records indicate that Crawford's Cafe was begun in 1924, while the Lowerys owned the building. A man by the name of Oscar Harper operated a dry goods store on the north side of the building while the cafe was on the south side.

Jack Lufkin and Robert Maxwell were among several residents who remembered Crawford's Cafe. Charles Lowrey said: "It was a small little restaurant, a tiny one. We went many times when we were teenagers. They had slot machines which paid off in dollars." Mirtis Anderson won a clock for eating so much soup. Her family still has that clock today.

In 1938, C. B. Crawford sold the building to Carey Powell from Walnut Hill. It's at this point that the records become a little clouded because of the overlap of owners and renters. Will and Collie Sharpless bought the restaurant and named it the Sweet Shop.

I received some correspondence from Martha and Johnny Sharpless regarding the restaurant and will quote what was written by Martha:

> This restaurant (Sweet Shop) was started by Johnny's first cousin in the mid 1930's. William Jones Sharpless and his wife, Collie Roan Sharpless, owned and operated this restaurant for many years. Knowing that Johnny's brother Roy had worked at the Sweet Shop, we were able to obtain lots of information from him. He said that the original location was only in the area where the small dining area is on the south side of the main dining room. Roy worked there from 1937 until he graduated from Escambia County High School in 1941. He said that there was a long counter with stools along the south side, with 2 booths in the back of the serving areas. Interestingly, he recalled that one of the most popular items on the menu was a delicious stew, with a cost of 25 cents for a full bowl and 15 cents for a half bowl. Also, on the menu were hamburgers, sandwiches and $1.00 plate lunches. Saturday was their busiest day, with the out-of-town folks coming into town to do their shopping. Sundays were for the local families coming in after church services. He said on the weekends, he would open up at 6 a.m. and stay for 10–12 hours. Their cook was a colored lady who really knew how to cook good food.

I'm not sure when Will and Collie sold the restaurant, but I recall a cousin of mine worked there in 1954–1955, and I know that the Sweet Shop was in the large dining room, as it is today. Will passed away in 1954 at the age of 62 and Collie lived to be 101 years old. I'm not certain when Will's niece, Louie Finch Sharpless Downey, owned and operated the Sweet Shop, but I recall being at a wedding party at the Country Club about 1966 and Louie Finch catered the affair. Louie Finch passed away Feb. 1, 1969, and was the daughter of Guy and Louie Sharpless, who lived on East Horner Street. Their homesite is now part of the First Presbyterian Church parking lot. Will and Collie lived directly behind the Episcopal Church.

When Louie Finch took over ownership, she made major changes in the restaurant. She was responsible for adding the handsome tin ceiling and making other major updating changes.

I've gotten some interesting tidbits from some Atmore residents. Elise Crook remembered the Sharpless family living upstairs above the restaurant before they built their house. Mrs. Herman Earle worked at Elmore's many years ago. She rode to town with a teacher and rode home on the bus. On Saturday mornings, she came on the bus from Walnut Hill and sat at the Sweet Shop until Elmore's opened. Mattie Lou Crook said that Mr. Sharpless was in competition with the City Cafe. He would count the number of customers coming in the door. Mr. Crook did the same thing. Robert Maxwell would buy one cent worth of bubble gum before going to the show. Mr. Sharpless was the cashier. James Forte remarked that the current private dining room used to be the Sweet Shop. A dry goods store was in the north side of the building until it was eventually bought for the Sweet Shop. WATM radio was located upstairs at one time. Willena Godwin went there to eat when she wanted something special. She had been in town one week when she went to eat there for the first time. She met the Ernest Ward principal and his wife who invited her in to dine with them. It was a memorable experience because the wife smoked in public, which was unusual at the time. H. C. Williams easily remembered the building when it was Crawford's Cafe with the counter and stools, hamburgers, and hotdogs. Charles Lowrey fondly remembered a date dessert that Will Sharpless had. He asked for the recipe and Collie said, "I don't give out recipes."

Haskew Middleton worked at the Sweet Shop in 1938, when Will owned the restaurant. He worked at Steele's Cash and Carry grocery store after school until 7 p.m., then he moved on to work at the Sweet Shop until closing. When I asked what time that was, Haskew replied, "I worked the curb until we closed which was when the last customer came, about 10 or 11 p.m." Coca-Colas were 5 cents and cheese sandwiches were a dime. For lunch and dinner, 15-cent stew was a popular choice. Many people would "drive up" and order a sandwich. Haskew was the carhop. Customers would drive up, toot their horns, and get curb service. He also gave curb service for ladies who wanted groceries, especially on Saturday mornings when they were still in their house coats![4]

The restaurant passed from Will and Collie Sharpless to Guy and Louie Sharpless, then to Louie Finch Sharpless Downey. At her death in 1969, James and Zema Pipkin bought the Sweet Shop but soon sold it to Jack and Claytie Dew. The Dews ran a successful restaurant and were known for their Italian fried chicken. In 1995, the restaurant was sold to a woman from the Florida panhandle.

Helen Rollo and her son Tom owned the property when it was the Wrangler Grill and Steak House, which was only open a short time before Tommy Gerlach purchased it and renamed the restaurant Gerlach's Main Street Grill. In 2005, Chris McElhaney bought out Gerlach, and three weeks later, Hurricane Ivan came through town and did major damage. The next owner was Jose Pinto who opened Pintoli's in February 2008. Other short-term restaurants located in the building were Nan's Main Street Cafe, Logie's Bakery and Cafe, and Parish Grill. The Parish Grill opened on August 14, 2014, and burned October 15, 2014. The building has been empty ever since.

One of Atmore's oldest citizens, Thera McCoy said, "The Sweet Shop was 'the' restaurant in town."

The two-story building had a flat roof with parapet and was on a poured concrete slab. It had double hung windows with brick arches. A remodeled storefront has a long rectangular recessed panel along the second floor, flanked by decorative wood vents. A second-floor eating area with a shed roof was added sometime in the 1980s. Most of the building is now in ruins from the 2014 fire. Still showing are the small brown and white tile floors.

120 South Main Street
ATMORE HARDWARE, WESTERN AUTO, DAY GALLERY

The original building which housed Atmore Hardware, which began in 1898, was at the corner of Main and Church streets, where the American Legion Building now stands. The hardware store was on the ground floor and the Masonic Lodge on the second. The company moved to its present location on South Main Street in 1904 when that building was completed. The Atmore Hardware was the town's first hardware, first undertaking establishment,

Atmore Hardware as recently renovated.

first Ford agency—selling the Model T—and first furniture store. It carried everything from cribs to coffins. Dr. A. P. Webb became president in 1904 and was followed by S. L. Rollins, E. S. Stone, and A. Pellar Webb Jr., who served until the store closed in 1994.[5]

Like many of the other early stores in Atmore, this one had wood floors and was heated by a coal burning potbelly stove which was located in the center of the store. From at least as early as the 1950s, the front north side held small appliances and gifts, and it was common to see Letha Webb sitting by the window or waiting on customers. James Wearren was the general manager and was employed by the company for over 50 years.

Mattie Lou Crook said that her crystal came from Atmore Hardware and cost $1 per stem. Many brides, including my mother and aunt, had their wedding china supplied by Atmore Hardware. These ladies took whatever pattern happened to be in stock and were glad to get it, especially those married during war years.

Between the hardware and the theater, the small building was where Gail Smith had his Western Auto store. Robert Maxwell and James Forte remembered Western Auto as did Haskew Middleton, who said: "Gail Smith was a young man. I thought it was so nice that a young man could own his own business and do good."

Lowell McGill mentioned something that no one else did, that there was a ten-pin bowling alley right next to the theater. He said you could hear the noise from it during the movies.

Also located in the Atmore Hardware building was the Day Gallery in 2008 and Smith Trading Company in 2014.

The building was built in 1904 and was composed of two stories with a parapet flat roof with limestone caps. It had fixed wood windows with two bays and decorative masonry work, double attached windows with corbelling, and faux pilasters at the second floor. There are second floor decorative brick panels and decorative rectangular panels with decorative diamond patterns. There are five arched windows with keystones at the top of each and a recessed sign area across the top which continues to the adjoining building with stacked brick above. There are two diamond vents. The adjacent building, north of the Hardware, had four glass transoms and one over the door. There is a gap in the building numbering system so the Western Auto building probably should have had an address of 118 South Main Street.

The new name chosen for the remodeled Atmore Hardware building is Encore at the Strand. The ground floor of Encore can be used for live music, wedding receptions, birthday parties, dances, group meetings, reunions, luncheons, or other rental options. Upstairs will feature a sound studio, dance studio, computer lab, and arts spaces.

116 South Main Street
STRAND THEATRE, LOWERY MERCANTILE

The site of the Strand Theatre also happens to be the site of Atmore's second store, the W. W. Lowery General Mercantile Store. Mr. Lowery was the fifth white man to settle in Atmore and opened this wooden general store. He also had the first store in town which was located where the Lowery House (*Atmore Advance* office today) once stood. Notice was taken of the decorative upper front of the store.[6]

Based on some information I had, Robert Maxwell did an exhaustive title search for the Strand Theatre. Mr. William Carney bought the Strand land and sold it to W. W. Lowery in 1896. He kept it until 1930 when it was deeded to his son Winton W. Lowery, who in 1931 deeded it to his wife, Florence Lowery. On June 16, 1936, the land was sold to R. E. Martin, founder of Martin Theaters. It passed on to Martin Theaters in 1948, to Creek Theatres, Inc in 1963, to Joey Kelley in 1991, to Strand Theatre, LLC (Wayne and Dawn Kelley) in 2002, and closed in November 2013 as the longest continually operating theater in Alabama.

As early as January 12, 1933, there was an advertisement for the Strand Theatre in the local newspaper. The show ran continuously from 3 until midnight on Saturdays. Regular admission was 15 cents for children and 30 cents for adults. After the Strand was sold to Martin,

The restored Strand Theatre in 2023.

the old theater was razed. During that time, an open-air theater was set up at the corner of Church and Main streets. Maxwell also said the theater burned in 1935, so that is probably the reason it was razed for a new building.

The new Strand Theatre was set to open in 1936. According to the *Atmore Advance*: "The new building will be 35 by 120 feet. It will have a ladies' and gentlemen's dressing room, a modern stage and dressing rooms for accommodation of road or vaudeville shows." On September 11, 1936, newspaper coverage continues: "New cushioned seats will be installed throughout the building, while in addition to the main floor, there will be two balconies, one for white and one for colored people. The front of the building is expected to make it one of the city's most attractive. The street facing will be in black onyx and trimmed appropriately in yellow." The new theater boasted "washed air conditioning" and a sprinkler system to put out fires. One of the most unusual items in the new building was the water fountain in the lobby. It was controlled by photo-electricity. When a patron bent over to drink from the fountain, a beam was broken from the electric eye, automatically causing water in the fountain to shoot upward.

Haskew Middleton always enjoyed the balcony at the theater. Whites went inside and then upstairs to the balcony. There was a partition in the middle, and the whites sat on the left and the blacks on the right (they having entered from the outside.) At this time in our history, before the Civil Rights Act was passed, it was customary for black patrons to sit in a special section in the balcony. Thus, the separate outside entrance for them. An adult could sit in the balcony for 15 cents. Haskew said, "If you had a girlfriend, it was kinda dark up there. You could also step out on the landing of the balcony and smoke."

Mirtis Anderson had an interesting tale about the theater. She said that after the theater was completely remodeled, inside and out, everybody came into town and went to the show on Saturday afternoon. One day while Lukie was away at war, Mirtis was "minding the store" and had her one-year-old son, Daulton, with her. While she was fitting shoes on a customer, Daulton disappeared. There was no air conditioning then so the doors were wide open. Daulton had wandered out the front doors and was nowhere to be found. Mrs. Leveret, who worked at the store, offered to go to the show and hunt for him. She started at the back and went row by row, finally finding Daulton on the front row. When he was brought back to the store, Mirtis took him to the back and ". . . when I got through with him, he decided he didn't want to go back to the show."[7]

In his weekly newspaper column in the *Atmore Advance*, Lowell McGill said of the Strand: "Young, pretty high school girls were hired as ushers to show patrons to their seats. These young ladies used a flashlight to guide you to a seat. The ushers were needed, because on some nights all the seats were taken. These girls walked you down the aisles with the flashlight beamed at the floor so as not to disturb those who were watching the movie."[8]

A bonus for the girls was that they got to watch the movie for free.

When asked to comment on the Strand, Thera McCoy said, "It's been there ever since I can remember." Robert Maxwell was one of the few who said he could remember when it was built in 1936. James Forte reminisced about the girl ushers, Saturday drawings when money was given away, the black outside staircase, and the outdoor theater. Edgar Norris remembered, not too fondly, falling asleep during the movie and his brothers leaving him there. With twelve children at home, he was not even missed. He said it cost ten cents to get in. In the 1950s, Lowell McGill's wife, Ouida, worked there when she was fifteen.

The Strand is a two-story, two-part commercial block building with a flat roof with projecting central parapet. The exterior walls are stucco with vinyl. There are four small windows across the top and four on the lower top. It has two double aluminum and glass doors. The exterior has been remodeled and covered with black and white tiles. As of 2023, the building was undergoing a total renovation to bring it back to its glory days.

114 and 112 South Main Street
RADIO SHACK, ANDERSON'S, GRIMSLEY AND SON, HAWT MESS, BETTY'S, HUSTLER'S MERCANTILE, ANDERSON LAW OFFICE

Lukie and Mirtis Anderson sat down with me in July, 1998, and expounded on their time in business on South Main Street. The building, now called the Anderson Building, is composed of two parts. Number 114, the southern half of the building was home to W. A. Grimsley and Son clothing store. Number 112 was Phillips Specialty Store, a

Left, the south side, and above, the empty north side of 114–112 South Main Street.

Ground floor of 112 South Main, now the Hawt Mess shop.

furniture store run by Mirtis's uncle, C. C. Everedge. Mr. J. F. Ballard owned both stores. Lukie said Ballard lived on Horner Street and had a Dodge touring car, which had an open roof and often carried a boat on top. He also had the ice plant in town. Lukie bought the northern half of the building from Ballard's daughter in 1936, at the ripe old age of nineteen. He later bought the southern part from Bernice Grimsley's son.

What became Anderson's Department Store originally had a Jewish name. So many Jewish people came in wanting handouts that they finally changed the name to Anderson's in 1952. Back when Everedge ran the store, he fired both Mirtis and Lukie. They would straighten up the store, and Everedge would come in and put everything on top of the counter. When Mr. Ballard found out, he got Lukie to come back and made Everedge leave the building. Everedge moved his stock to Brewton, and Lukie had to start over from scratch. George Bowab, another local merchant, said he'd never make it. Lukie had other ideas and put them into practice and made the store a success. One of his early "tricks" was that after he sold a pair of shoes, he would put the box back on the shelf so it wouldn't look empty. He opened the store in 1936 and closed it in 2000, after sixty-four years.

James Forte mentioned that his wife worked at Grimsley's Department Store for a while. Haskew Middleton recalled Grimsley's going-out-of-business sale which lasted for five years, with new merchandise coming in the back door every day. The 1949 *Advance* in its ad for Grimsley's said, "Atmore's Most Modern Store."

James Anderson, Lukie and Mirtis's grandson, said the two buildings mirrored each other and had a combined 10,000 square feet. He said, "When my grandfather bought the building in the 1960s, he decided he was going to break a walk-through to have a men's side over here and a women's side over there, and a shoe department in the back which stretched across both sides."[9]

When Daulton Anderson, Lukie's other son, moved back to Atmore in the 1970s, he realized the need for a store which sold electronics and opened Radio Shack in the southern side of the building.

Something special in front of the north side of the building is the trapezoid-shaped area which is covered in a lovely cornflower blue and white tile carpet with a repeating continuous design border. It is an example of the commonly used one-inch tile.[10]

The building was probably constructed in the 1910–1925 time frame. It is two stories with a parapet flat roof within a two-part commercial block. It has a recessed sign area, two arched windows, and two recessed diamond-shaped decorative vents. Eleven small transom windows are across the top of the first floor. In the 1960s, the facade was added above the storefront and refaced with vinyl and an aluminum and glass door. The front two entrances each have a bay, flanked by glass display windows.

The store building has been home to Betty's in the south part and Hustler's Mercantile in the north half. David Anderson had his law office in the rear of the building. Currently, Hawt Mess is open in the 112 South Main Street portion.

108 South Main Street
ESCAMBIA DRUG STORE

Remember cherry Cokes, grilled-cheese sandwiches with a chocolate milkshake, root beer floats, and a scoop of ice cream or cup of coffee that cost a nickel? Remember the long marble counter of the soda fountain with the 12 stools firmly planted on the floor? What about the booths with their black table tops which had many students' names carved into them? Remember sitting in one of those booths with your special someone, drinking one drink with two straws? Remember trying to see how many people you could cram into a booth meant for four? Remember going to the soda fountain at the drug store to see and be seen? Those were the heydays of Escambia Drug Store.

Ken Barnett, the pharmacist until his death in 2016, thought Escambia Drugs was the oldest establishment working under the same name in Atmore and maybe in the county. The building was built by Mr. J. T. Ballard, and the store was established and opened about 1914 by Dr. W. R. Holley. Holley actually sold and got the store back several times. Eventually, Winston Dunn bought the store in 1933 and was there until he died in 1954 or 1955. James Nall and Henry Lowery then ran the store for Mrs. Dunn until 1957. Barnett entered the scene in 1957 when Lowery opened Greenlawn Pharmacy that same year. In 1985, Ken Barnett bought the business and Wayne Barnett joined his father.

Ken Barnett actually began his career at Escambia

Drug Store at age thirteen when he worked behind the soda fountain selling ice cream. Asked about the closing of the soda fountain, Ken said: "It was just one of those things. In the later years it was not profitable due to the help we had to have. Tom Kelly had Reid Drug and he and Escambia Drugs closed their soda fountains about the same time. Claude Bristow continued his for a while."

One of the unusual features of Escambia Drugs was their drive up service. Customers would drive up, toot the horn, and someone would come out and take the order. There were accordion doors across the front of the store, so driving up was relatively easy. This service was stopped during World War II. Prescriptions were delivered all over town by bicycle in the 1940s–1960s.

With the soda fountain gone, a group of Atmore men descended on the back room of the drug store and formed their own coffee club. They would meet in the mornings to talk. Some would come back in the afternoon. Some of those men, namely Dick Jones, J. D. "Grinny" Jones, and Burton Smith, were rather gullible, and it was easy to

Escambia Drug Store, center.

pull one over on them. What follows is one of the great stories of Atmore.

Someone came up with the idea of building a domed stadium in Flomaton which would be as large as the Superdome. Flomaton was selected as the site because of its central location. The dome would be the playing venue for area high school football games. The three above mentioned men were convinced by the other men that this was going to happen The tricksters even began bringing in other people to elaborate on the story. A city councilman came in and told the men how much money the city was going to give. Bill Zelm, who was with the power company, told how much he figured the electricity would be. This went on for months and months. They were even told by Ken Barnett that when he went to Brewton on business, he saw bulldozers cleaning the site (present-day Hurricane Park). The joke was going along fine until one day Dick Jones was at the drug store having coffee when County Commissioner Weldon Vickrey came in. Dick jumped on him about spending county money for a domed stadium. Weldon said that no one had told him the county commission was building a domed stadium, and he was going to Brewton to see what was going on and why he hadn't been informed. To keep Weldon from storming Brewton, the men finally had to break down and admit that the whole thing was a hoax. It was a good and harmless joke that kept many Atmore citizens in good humor for three or four months.[11]

Stories and memories of Escambia Drug Store abound. Haskew Middleton told of his mother ordering a dose of castor oil flavored with a Coke and having a black boy on a bicycle bring it to the house. They would deliver Cokes if you called it in back then. The boy would ride on his bike with a tray in the palm of his hand and the glass of Coke on said tray. They would return later to collect the glass.

Larry Fischer, a member of the unofficial drug store men's coffee group, related a tale about watermelons which was rather fishy, pun intended. This story took place in the 1960s. Alton Tennant planted watermelons to sell and these melons caused all kind of havoc in Atmore—even to the police department. The story started at the soda fountain. The men knew that Alton loaded his trunk with melons and would give a few away. One Sunday morning, Ken Barnett called Alton and asked him to come and bring some watermelons. Alton was suspicious because it was Ken who called and on a Sunday. He decided to have his own fun. The watermelons were removed from the trunk and a stuffed leaping bobcat was substituted. When Alton arrived at the drug store, he parked right in front so everyone could see him. The men got Alton to come to the back of the store, and one slipped out to steal himself a watermelon. When he opened the trunk and saw the bobcat, it scared him so silly he fled the scene. Even Johnny Jones, First National Bank president, went out to steal himself a melon. He got as far as the theater before he realized what was going on. Police Chief Clarence Bryars went out to get himself a watermelon and discovered the bobcat. You can imagine what these men thought when they saw the stuffed cat. You can also imagine what Alton was thinking when he knew the men were being faced with the menacing cat. Finally, the police chief came back into the drug store and wouldn't let Alton take his car home. Instead, he took it to the police station and played the trick on the men working there. All was well until Charlie Shanks, who was on the force, was scared so badly that he ran into the side of a police car and bent the door. That put an end to stealing watermelons.

Elise Crook mentioned that dentist Dr. Zollie Mims had his office above the drug store. When he pulled teeth, for fun he would throw them out the window. Patricia Crook Threadgill remembered the soda fountain and going in to buy cosmetics. This was back in the day when drug stores sold drugs and cosmetics and grocery stores sold groceries. The cosmetic counter was a favorite place to check out the newest perfumes and Revlon lipstick.

James Forte recalled the folding doors which would open all the way to expose the entire store (depicted in 1930s street scene on page x). The ice cream box was on wheels and would be rolled out to the door or even outside to attract customers. Byard Swift commented that they sold only chocolate and vanilla ice cream. Others said the box had holes for four flavors of ice cream and that they were always all full.

Edgar Norris had another tall tale. A manikin was put in the back of the drug store, and Mr. Clarence Bryars, the police chief, was called one night about a burglary in progress at the drug store. He rushed across the tracks and into the dark store where he saw a figure and proceeded to tackle it. The rest of the story ended in a fit of laughter. Because of the above-mentioned watermelon prank, I suspect this was a set up to have fun with the chief.

An old advertisement for Escambia Drug Store said: "Atmore's Leading Drug Store—Regular meals, plate lunches, short orders. Try our special breakfast for 17 cents."

The building was constructed in 1914 by Mr. Ballard with brick and was covered with stucco on the second story. It has a flat roof. There is no visible decorative brickwork. There are three window openings. The glass storefront was added in the 1960s when the large accordion doors were removed.

One of the prettiest tile floors in Atmore is that in Escambia Drug Store. Those tiles are much larger and more colorful than others in town. They measure 7½ inches square and are obviously old, but we don't know how old. The store underwent a major remodeling in 1951. An old photograph shows the tiles in place in 1959, but they could have been laid at any time before that. The border is of two shades of olive green and white and is a combination of designs with each tile making up part of the center design. The rest of the floors are white, light and dark gray, and bright yellow.[12] Lance's Outlet is the current occupant.

102 and 100 South Main Street
WE CARE, CARNEY MILL COMMISSARY, DRESS SHOP, FRED'S, ELMORE'S

The building on the corner of Main and Nashville has a long and storied history. To one generation, it was the location of Carney Mill Company Commissary which opened in 1876, and, to another, it housed Elmore's Five and Dime. The current generation will recall it as We Care. Whatever occupies the space now, it is an interesting building. It appears to have been three adjacent buildings, entirely separate of each other, but constructed at the same time. All three have recessed sign areas on the second story and double stacked decorative brick at the top. Both vertical and horizontally laid brick is in a framing design. It is not possible to see them now, but the building has window openings and storefront opening on two facades with a large transom opening along the front facade which has been boarded up. There are three bays with pilasters separating the bays and the front has been covered with tile. Currently, all three buildings have been opened up and are occupied by We Care. Because of the layout of the building, it is difficult to tell where stores have been located in the past as some times there was one store, and, at others, two or three stores in the location. This also has the street numbering of stores off.

According to Charles and Velma Bosenberg, Clyde Stokes had a dress store upstairs. Before then, the upstairs was empty and was used for Halloween parties. They said

We Care Thrift Store.

it was dark and "cobwebby." Nell Thomas also mentioned Stokes as having a store there. I can vaguely remember the Stokes' store, but thought it was downstairs. Memories are hard to trust so I may be mistaken.

Helen Lumpkin had some interesting first hand information on the building when Carney Mill had it. She said that downstairs had two connecting buildings. Carney Mill Company had low-price things on the south side. Helen worked upstairs in the beauty shop on the south side. Mrs. Nelson had a dry goods and beautiful gifts on the north. Carney's store was considered the nicest store between Montgomery and Mobile with lighted cases, china, and crystal. Adeline Gomilla ran the south side down stairs. Hats were upstairs. Helen went to beauty school and worked upstairs and ran Mrs. Gomilla's beauty shop. In 1941, she was in the Looking Glass Beauty Shop with Nell Wise.

James Forte and Bill Chapman recalled Fred's on the north side in later years. Ellie Bailey added that Byron Tims had Fred's. Cliff Frazier said Tommy Stallworth worked for Carney Mill and then had a dry goods store. Zolan Middleton had a men's store and Frazier and Peanut McDonald worked there. Haskew Middleton said that Zolan Middleton had men and boys downstairs with women's clothing upstairs. He moved his store from Nashville to Main Street.

Byard Swift discussed the Carney complex as a commissary with food items run by James Nall's father. The north side of the building was the largest part and held the department store which was run by a man named Clingo. The post office was located in the back.

Edgar Norris had some stories in his memory bank that no one else had. Ray Lassiter had a sports store with hunting equipment, and Lee's Music Store was there but did not last long. Main Street Arcade and the Economy Shop were also tenants as were Vic's, New York Fashions, Factory Connection, and Betty's Women's Clothes.

This author has many fond memories of Elmore's, which was run by Johnny Hoehn. To me, as a child, the store was huge and a true child's paradise. I would walk by the store every time I went to my granddaddy's store on North Main and would stop and look in the windows. Since I didn't have any money of my own, I didn't go inside unless an adult was with me, at least not until I was older. I do remember walking in and looking at the goldfish. They were in little plastic bags which were filled with water and were stapled to a board. I never had any goldfish but always was excited to watch them swim around in their bags.

By far, the best thing about Elmore's to me was the sewing section. When I was seven, my grandmother taught me how to cross stitch and later embroider. She would copy designs on cup towels, and I would work on them in the afternoons after swimming lessons at the city pool. Eventually, I discovered you could buy items which were already stamped and that was the aisle I would head to. They had cup towels, pillowcases, pot holders, baby bibs, and other assorted items. It was sheer delight to pick out an item and then go to the section of thread and pick out the colors I wanted to work the design in. For only five cents a skein, it was a relatively cheap hobby. I was very careful to not tangle the thread and would keep it to do with future projects. To this day, I still have a small box of my early-days thread as well as some that my mother had. I'm sure they are rotten after sixty or seventy years, but they are a reminder of wonderful summer days. As I was cleaning out Mother's house after she died, I found that first cup towel I made. She had carefully packed it away for safekeeping. I also have one of the early embroidered potholders. Elmore's was my favorite store.

107 (109) West Nashville Avenue
HELEN'S, THAMES BARBER, BATESON'S TOO, UNITED BANK

This building has been used as one business location or divided in half for two different businesses. Because of that, confusion is evident about correct addresses.

Byard Swift probably goes back the farthest with Thompson Kearley selling water and farm pumps. When I spoke with Helen Lumpkin in 2006, she said that Tommy Stallworth owned the building. She had her beauty shop in one side, and Otis Thames had a barber shop on the other side. Nancy Williams eventually bought Helen out when she was ready to retire. The building was also home to Bateson's Too, an annex to their main shop. One picture

United Bank's Community Development offices.

made in 1997 shows the building with a huge sign saying "Signs" across the front but not sure what it was inside. Another picture has Youth printed on the glass but no explanation for it either.

As of 2021, United Bank had the full building for its Community Development services and used numbers 109 A and 109 B. The building has two front entrances.

James Forte said the second building behind We Care once housed the Kearley store of farm pumps. He also said Gail Smith built it for Western Auto and that it has been a book store and fabric store. High school yearbooks, phone books, and city directories list a video store, Karate Studio, Bargain TV Sales and Service, and Shopper's Bazaar as tenants.

Neither building has any outstanding architectural elements. It is a basic store building with large windows on the front. Some pictures show metal awnings, some fabric canopies, and some bare storefronts.

111 West Nashville Avenue
GAS STATIONS, BRANTLEY TIRES, JUS BECAUSE, GATHER

While the building next door may be bland architecturally, this one certainly is not. This former gas station has a story to tell. In the early days of filling stations, they tended to be messy and unattractive, with the result that many people did not want them in visible spots. Pure Oil Company decided to take the bull by the horns and change this image. They developed a cheap, attractive design in the Tudor Revival style. It became their corporate trademark, beginning in 1927. The design was used all over the country, including in Atmore. White-painted brick was used on the buildings. They mostly had steeply pitched gabled roofs originally covered with blue terra cotta tile. The buildings had brick chimneys at each end of the gables with a large metal "P" near the top. The style was designed to be, and was, aesthetically pleasing for every town. Drivers also knew, when they recognized one in the distance, exactly what kind of service and gas they would find.

Byard Swift and Edgar Norris both recalled a WOCO Pep gas station at that location. It could be that W. E. "Red" Lumpkin had that brand and switched over to Pure and was given an opportunity to have one of their buildings. However, this is doubtful because Red worked for R. Leon Jones until Jones sold to Robert Long. It's more probable that someone else ran the

Red Lumpkin's Pure Gas Station, now Gather Restaurant.

Bateson's Furniture.

WOCO Pep station. A metal drive-thru was added to the front facade in the 1960s by Red.

Even before Red had his gas station, the Brantleys had Brantley Tires there before they moved to North Main Street. Ellie Bailey commented that Mr. Wise had a peanut machine in back where the tires were. Carl Anderson added that Dennis Simmons had a car repair at the site and someone mentioned Williams Realty.

In more recent times, the building was home to a ladies boutique, Jus Because, and now Gather. Rob Faircloth and Terrence Breckenridge are the ones to thank for rescuing another old and beautiful building that was falling into disrepair. Even with additions made to enlarge it enough for a restaurant, the overall shape of the building, with the distinctive chimneys and front windows, is still there, as is the decorative letter "P" on each chimney.

100 South Trammell Street
BATESON'S FURNITURE, JONES FORD, GECA

John Webb said that R. Leon Jones had the Ford dealership at this location in 1927. The Alberts lived next door on Trammell Street. That house caught fire and burned. Hugo Esneul's son-in-law got the business when Jones died in 1954. Byard Swift said that Jim Bell had furniture in the building during World War II. Bateson's took over in 1946 but in another location, not moving here until after A&P moved to their new location on West Nashville.

I don't remember who was in the building at the time, but I can remember going inside to buy 45rpm records which were in large bins at the front of the store. The front was unusual because of its chopped off entrance. James Forte said that R. Leon Jones had it removed at an angle so that gas pumps could be placed there. It became a distinctive feature of the building.

Back to the history of Bateson's. The company started out on South Main Street, next to Burger King, on land owned by Thera Kelly McCoy and Betty Kelly Luttrell. Randy Luttrell purchased the site from the Kelly sisters.

In 1947, Randolph Luttrell was discharged from the Army. He and Les McCoy married the Kelly sisters. Les agreed to help with the furniture store and proposed use of the McCoy Building. He went to Atlanta to the furniture market and was told he couldn't buy furniture because his store did not have a name. He decided on the spot to name it Bateson's because that was his middle name. The store was in several locations before it ended up in the R. Leon Jones Motor Company building. Bateson's closed in 2006 and was sold in 2007. Some remodeling was done and then GECA, Greater Escambia Council for the Arts, moved in and has delighted citizens with their theatrical productions.

The building was built sometime in the 1920s. It has a flat roof with round projected parapet. The entrance is angled and permanently closed with a main entrance on the Trammell Street side. There are several rows of very decorative brickwork which is enhanced by different color paint. There are decorative brick pilasters as well as stone lintels and sills. Vertical stone strips run the length of the building on either side of the entrance bay.

101 North Trammell Street
Currie's Gin, Central Farm Supply

Currie's Gin first opened in 1916 and closed in 1984. This is a one-story building with a wing and is freestanding concrete blocks with a flat roof and a parapet on the main bay. There are four interior brick chimneys with limestone caps, small fixed metal windows, one garage entrance with loading bay, and sits on a concrete block foundation. The six metal silos are grouped as one and date to about 1940.

James Forte said that Currie's was located right by the railroad tracks and had a side track where grain was loaded. Dan Currie is the one who eventually sold the business. In its heyday, the streets would be lined for blocks with wagons full of picked cotton waiting their turn to have it unloaded and ginned. The hum of the gins could be heard all over town. The streets were lined with cotton fluff, and cotton lint made its way to screen windows of the homes located in or near the downtown area. Cotton was big business and much of the economy depended on the local cotton gins. Currie's also sold seed and baby chicks. I can remember being taken there by my grandfather to watch the cotton being ginned and then going inside to see the baby chicks. Since they had a chicken yard at their house, Currie's was where they went to purchase the babies each year.

Fall was always an exciting time of the year and having gins running to capacity at all of the local gins brought in lots of people and certainly aided the economy. Local

The Buildings

100 North Trammell Street
GRAHAM-BROOKS

Anyone who had any kind of business in Atmore which dealt with food was probably a customer of Graham-Brooks. They were the only wholesale grocer in Atmore and supplied most of those businesses. John Webb was a storehouse of information on Atmore history because of his age and the many years he lived in Atmore, most of them being at the Webb house on North Main Street. He also had a quick and accurate mind and loved to talk about the old times here. He knew both Mr. Graham and Mr. Brooks personally and said Leon Brooks was from Brewton and Tom Graham lived in Atmore.

Mattie Lou Crook, one of the owners of City Cafe, said that they bought their store groceries from Graham-Brooks. Pellar Webb would come for their grocery list and bring the items back to the cafe. I don't know if that delivery service was arranged by Graham-Brooks, the Crooks, or Pellar, but it worked out well for all concerned. merchants benefited as did the farmers and cotton pickers.

Central Farm Supply once occupied the facility and now Atmore Farm & Garden still sells seeds. Additionally, they supply bedding plants, small trees, house plants, gift items, and most importantly, advice on all things plants. And, oh yes, you can still take your grandchildren there to see the baby chicks!

Top left, Atmore Farm & Garden. Below, Graham-Brooks.

John Shiver reminded me that Leon Brooks had a law office in the building. I had forgotten that until he mentioned it, then I remembered going there as a child when my grandfather gave me a piece of land and had me sign some papers about it.

James Forte had some information about Ernest Steele, or "Big Steele" as he was called. Local freight came in on the train two times a day with railway express coming on passenger trains. Mr. Steele had contracts to deliver with L&N and Frisco, mostly to stores in town and the nearby area. He had a gray Belgian horse and a wagon which he used for deliveries. The horses were kept in the Graham-Brooks building. In the early 1930s, he finally bought a truck for his deliveries. Jack Lufkin also remembered the draft horses staying there and making deliveries.

Virginia Sharpless said that Martha and Johnny Sharpless had the Decorating Center in the building, having moved there from the old Albert's Restaurant which was by the trestle. Keith Castleberry has an Edward Jones office in the building at this time.

This is a slightly irregular U-shaped brick freestanding building with a flat roof and terra cotta coping. Double hung windows have limestone sills throughout and a central entry with wood transom and wood surrounds. Decorative brick panels are all around the facade. One of the bays on the front leg of the "U" was converted to a commercial storefront in the 1970s and retains the massive stone lintel. There are two exterior brick chimneys and a brick foundation.

110 West Louisville Avenue
MARTIN CONSTRUCTION

Not much is known about this building except that it is often included as part of the 100 North Trammell Graham-Brooks building. It was home to Premier Glass at one time, and now Martin Construction calls it home.

The one distinguishing thing about this building is the stone lintel and the engraving on it: "Hallelujah!!! E Pluribus Unum Ha! Ha! Ha!" which was done by Farrar Barnett. It is understood that the Ha! Ha! Ha! stands for "Hallelujah! Hallelujah! Hallelujah!"

Right side of Graham-Brooks.

Crossing the Tracks

If one thing stands out about Atmore, it is the train tracks running through the middle of town. Those tracks are the lifeblood of the town and, in fact, gave it birth. Railroads were built in Alabama before the Civil War, but construction all but stopped because of the scarcity of materials. In places, tracks were dug up and shipped to more vital areas. After the war, construction resumed and tracks were laid from Pollard to the Tensaw. Later, the ferries which transported trains across rivers were replaced by railroad bridges.

Where people live, supplies are needed. Trains make arrangements to stop and leave those supplies. Such was the case for William Larkin Williams, who lived just south of what is now the center of Atmore. The drop-off for his supplies became known as Williams' Station. Try to imagine the town in 1870, only five years after the Civil War. The small Williams' Station had dirt streets, a railroad stop of sorts, a store which contained a post office, and one house. That same year, a sawmill was started, and more workers moved to the area.

It took the arrival of William Marshall Carney, with his timber and turpentine industries, to really draw people to the small town. In 1897, the name was changed to Atmore, in honor of C. P. Atmore, the general ticket agent for the Louisville and Nashville Railroad. That is where we get the moniker of "the L&N tracks" that we use today. These tracks run almost parallel to U.S. Highway 31.

I was trying to figure out when I last rode on the L&N tracks when it suddenly dawned on me. I pulled out my trusty diary to make sure I was correct, and I was. My college roommate, who lived in Birmingham, had asked me to be in her wedding. To get there, I took the train. Not just any train, mind you, but the Humming Bird! The date was September 6, 1968. Just a year later the sleek train was retired from service as rail travel began to fall off.

I remember watching the Humming Bird travel through Atmore, much as later citizens watched Amtrak. It was something to see. The engine was a deep blue and cream with red trim, and the carriages were blue and stainless steel. It was sleek and modern for its day. The Humming Bird began its route in 1947 as a no-frills train that was affordable to the general public. It operated between Cincinnati and New Orleans, with Chicago being added later. It had only the engine, five coaches, a diner, and lounge car. By the early 1950s, Pullman service and sleeping cars had been added. The only problem was that it did not stop in Atmore. You had to go to Flomaton to catch it.

Atmore's other train was the Frisco. This train came along about 1914 and

went from Pensacola, Florida, to Frisco City, Alabama. Its route was moved by about a mile to come almost exactly through town when the overhead trestle was built. I asked my friend Sheryl Vickery for some information because I knew her grandfather had a part in building the current trestle. She said that William Henry "Willie" Wise owned many acres of land, especially in the McCullough area, and was a farmer. He furnished the dirt for the trestle, bringing it from McCullough with a horse and wagon. He was paid $1 per load, and the project took 25,000 loads of dirt. An interesting fact about Mr. Wise is that he married his wife in 1894 when she was only fifteen and he was twenty-seven. They had sixteen children. Another little tidbit about the Frisco is related to me and not the Wise family. When I was in first grade in Pensacola in 1953, my class took a train ride from Pensacola to Cantonment. My father was one of the chaperones and took along his 16mm movie camera. What fun to look today at those old movies of my first train ride. Parents met the train and drove us back to school.

In 1895, Morris Slater, a black man also known as Bill McCoy, but better known as Railroad Bill, began riding L&N trains between Flomaton and Bay Minette. Of course, that took him right through Atmore. He was notorious for the large rifle he carried and the robberies he committed. He would rob trains and steal goods, then sell them to people along the tracks at much reduced prices, and even give some away. This man was said to have supernatural powers because he could escape into nowhere and often an animal would appear close by. Posses were formed with rewards out for his capture, but he always managed to escape.

Railroad Bill was responsible for twelve murders, including those of Deputy James Stewart in Bay Minette and Sheriff Ed McMillan of Brewton. The latter's murder so outraged the public that a bounty of $1,250 (about $45,000 today) was raised for the capture of Bill. Unfortunately for him, Railroad Bill made a fatal mistake on March 7, 1896, when he sauntered into Atmore's Tidmore and Ward's store on Ashley Street, where he bought some cheese and crackers. The desperado walked outside, sat on a barrel, and proceeded to eat his snack. His mistake was that he did not bring his ever-present rifle. One of the men in the store recognized Bill and shot him in the back, killing him.

The body was tied to a board and put on display in Atmore. It was then carried to Brewton where it was embalmed and again displayed, with citizens paying the huge sum of 25 cents to view the body. Some even paid 50 cents to have their picture taken with it. From there, the corpse was transported to Montgomery and then south to Pensacola where it was buried in St. James Cemetery.

Railroad Bill became something of a folklore hero with many ballads written about him. These became especially popular during the 1950s and 1960s and were played almost as much as the "Ballad of Davy Crockett." A musical play was written and performed in New York, and he is included in many books. He was often called the Robin Hood of the Rails. Part of one of the versions of the ballad goes: "Railroad Bill, Railroad Bill. He never worked and he never will. And it's ride, ride, ride. Railroad Bill's a mighty mean man. Shot the light out of the brakeman's hand. Railroad Bill, up on a hill, Lightin' a cigar with a ten dollar bill. And it's ride, ride, ride."

108 West Louisville Avenue
ELITE BARBER SHOP, DANNIE'S BEAUTY SHOP

Jack Beck said of the Elite Barber Shop, "It was owned by Herman Lewis and was on East Louisville Avenue." Byard Swift volunteered that Herman built the building to house his barber shop. It had an area behind the barber shop area which was used by customers who wanted a shower with their shave. That area was eventually closed off and was last Dannie's Beauty Shop.

Going into the Elite today is like stepping back in time. The floors are covered in small, probably one inch octagonal tiles, typical of what is found in most tiled barber shops. What grabs attention is the large barber chair with the elaborate metal footrest. It is indeed a work of art. Other familiar sights are the glass bottles which hold shampoo and tonic and the familiar smells. Gone, however, are the straight razors and razor strops, casualties of safety and sanitation standards of today. One jewel which remains is the barber pole outside that quickly tells anyone passing by what is inside the building.

The Elite, which was probably built in the 1920s or 1930s, is a one-story brick commercial building with a parapet flat roof with terracotta coping on the front and sides. A decorative brick panel is above the 1960s era glass storefront, and it is on a poured concrete foundation.

The Elite Barber Shop building dates to the early twentieth century.

104–102 West Louisville Avenue
DR. THORNBLOOM, NEW ME CENTER, D&G FINEST CUTS

So many businesses have come and gone in these two addresses over the years that it is impossible to tell what was where. Most have been short-term tenants and turnover has been rapid.

The best estimate for construction of the building is 1920, but it could be older. We do know that Abbie Stewart built her house on South Main Street where First National Bank is now located in 1901. Previously, she had lived on the northwest corner of Louisville and Main, the site of the building under discussion. The current Heavenly Escape building on North Main was built in 1920. So it stands to reason that our building falls between 1901 and 1920, but that is still a large span of years. One thing which pushes it more towards 1920, are the lovely tile floors in front of the entryway. Others of the same design were installed in stores in the early 1920s, so these probably were as well.

The building is a two-story brick construction with a flat roof. A recessed entrance bay forms a trapezoid with slanted walls and doors for each entrance. There are four double hung windows with limestone sills on the second floor back of the building and four on the Louisville side.

Known tenants have been Dr. Cecil Thornbloom and his chiropractic office, New Me Center Beauty Shop, D&G Finest Cuts, Shane Cooper attorney's office, Bailey Communications Services, Risque Boutique, Southern Link, Agnes's Beauty Shop, T. J.'s Hair Repair Beauty Shop, Communications (cell phones), and Infinity Health Care Management.

Many tenants have occupied these two addresses.

100 West Louisville Avenue
DRS. ROGERS, THOMAS, TREHERNE, MILLSON, PEAVY

Many offices have been located upstairs in this building. Some have had a 100 North Main Street address and some a 100 West Louisville Avenue address. Most people I queried just knew they were upstairs and had no idea what the street address was. The names below are added to this group while some listed for the Main Street or 102 Louisville address may have actually been upstairs at 100 West Louisville.

Dr H. H. Rodgers Sr. had a dental office here, according to John Webb and Margarette Earle. Nell Thomas said Dr. James Thomas had an office upstairs, as did Otis Wise Insurance. James Forte reported Dr. Treherne being upstairs as did Byard Swift. Lowell McGill added Dr. Millson's dental office to the mix. Going way back, Dr. Julian Peavy was also in the upstairs of 100 West Louisville. Serenity Heart Home Health Care and Edward Jones have been mentioned as upstairs at one time.

101–103 North Main Street
TIGER LILY, REID DRUG, MANY MORE

Just after crossing the railroad tracks, on the northwest corner, is one of the most confusing buildings in downtown. So many businesses have been located both upstairs and downstairs that it is sometimes difficult to remember which part of the building housed what. Again, memories often get confused.

This is a two-part commercial block two-story building with a flat roof with cornice and narrowly spread delicate brick corbelling with one brick recessed panel beneath it. It is on a poured concrete slab foundation and has fixed double hung windows with stone sills. The corner building has a shorter two-story rear building. There is a recessed entrance toward the rear of the wing. By far, the most outstanding feature of this building are the fantastic tile floors.

I was walking down Main Street one day and had to stop for a train. I noticed remodeling going on at the building on the corner of Main and Louisville, the site of the former Tiger Lily that was once a baby and children's boutique. The door was open, and I peeked in. What a shock to see some of the most beautiful tiled floors ever, right there before my eyes. The new owners, Chris and Brandy Fehr, were working on several projects when I stuck my head in the door and asked what they were going to do with the floors. I won't go into details of what they said, but my sad face and puppy dog eyes, along with a few choice words about how beautiful they would be if restored, evidently did the trick. After much intensive labor, the results are spectacular and the floors are the highlight of the building and a credit to the two young entrepreneurs.

The floors are in two shades of blue and white. The hexagon-shaped cornflower blue tiles are formed into a flower design with a dark blue center. All along the outside edge is a border, nine tiles wide, which defines the perimeter (see photo, page 114). These gorgeous floors were covered with a covering which had been glued down. It was truly a labor of love for the Fehrs to spend the time it took to strip the glue and clean the tiles. But, oh, how wonderful they look! They also bring some of the history of Atmore to life. Many thanks to them for having the heart to take the right path and not the easy one. The building is now Trace Patrick Apparel, a men's and boy's clothing store, owned by Hunter Mosley.

I spoke with Kevin Claussen about the old Reid Drug building. He said it was built in 1920, when the tile was laid. It is currently covered by laminate and is not visible. More than likely, it is the same as at Tiger Lily since they are next door to each other and the buildings were built about the same time.[13]

Annie Ruth Whitten said that Tony Albert had Rex Sporting Goods in the corner building. I can remember buying textbooks and gym suits there in the 1960s. According to Elise Crook, Dr. Millson had his dental practice upstairs, and there was a barber shop in the back. Robert Maxwell agreed with Elise and said it was the Elite Barber

The old Reid Drug Building.

Shop with J. A. Reid as the barber. Maxwell said Reid was a very religious man and if you wanted to get a haircut, you had to listen to a sermon. He would make a point by waving a comb in your face. The whole building was owned by Dr. J. F. Peavy. James Forte said Herman Lewis had a barber shop there but moved into the building next to Graham-Brooks.

Byard Swift said Reid's barber shop was next door to Reid Drug Store. Even further back in time, Marcia Webb Pepperman said Abbie Stewart opened Abbie's Millinery Shop and had a boarding house where Reid Drug eventually was located. Stewart later moved across the railroad tracks to South Main Street. Edward Jones and Mark Brown Investment were also located in the building.

John Webb said that Mr. J. A. Reid owned the drug store at 103 North Main Street, but that Beck Green and Guy Sharpless were the pharmacists. They kept the name of Reid Drug when Guy Sharpless owned the building because it was already an established name. Vera Lufkin said that, in later years, Reid Drug Store had a soda fountain where she sat with friends and had a Coke. Tom Kelly bought the drug store from Beck Green.

Joel and Louise Day remembered that Guy Sharpless and Beck Green owned the drug store and Louise Day, Voncile Gulsby, and Agnes Brown worked there. Ice cream was made in-house, and people would come in for ice cream and milk shakes. Harry Nall had a grocery on South Main Street and sold donuts. They would get donuts, come to Reid to buy ice cream, put it on the donuts, and sit down to a delicious feast. The Days said that on Saturday nights, people walked the sidewalks and window shopped. There were tables and chairs in back of the drug store, and people would come in for coffee or ice cream before the store closed about 9.

The building was also, at one time, a fitness center owned by Robert Earle Brantley and run by his wife. Jack Lufkin mentioned that Sharpless got the Browning franchise and sold guns and shells and other sporting goods in the drug store. Later, he sold them through Rex Sporting Goods. Tony and Toad Albert had a sandwich shop. Several people commented on this but there was no consensus about which building it was in.

The building has also been home to offices for dentists Drs. Ponder and Millson, Sisters (which sold gifts, linens, cards, and stationery and was run by Brenda Wade), James Wilson's bookstore, Main Street Fitness Center, and Heavenly Escape Salon and Spa.

This building appears to have been built at the same time as 103 because their upper facades are identical.

105 North Main Street

MAXWELL-HALEY, CINDERELLA SHOPPE, TOT SHOP

The best person left in Atmore to give information on the Maxwell-Haley Building, also known as W. R. Maxwell & Sons, was Robert Maxwell, who was one of the sons of W. R. Maxwell. According to Robert, Maxwell's office was in the back room of what became Bristow's Pharmacy. At 3 in the afternoons, he sat in front of Bristow's, waiting for Bob Long and H. C. Williams to get off from work so they could play golf.

The south side of the building contained World War I veteran A. L. Gandy's shoe shop. The north side was the Cinderella Shoppe which was owned by Adeline Patterson Gomilla in partnership with Mrs. J. T. Peavy, the third wife of Dr. Peavy. W. R. Maxwell moved into the south side and Snookie Anderson into the north side, 107, with the Tot Shop. Maxwell recounted that the Jaycees had an Automobile Awareness Program and borrowed a casket from the funeral home and put it on the Main Street sidewalk between W. R. Maxwell and the Tot Shop. There was a sign in front which said, "Look inside—the next victim." There was a mirror inside, and when the person looked in, they saw their face reflected back. This upset Snookie when she saw it because she had just lost her husband in July 1956. The coffin was soon returned to the funeral home.

Annie Ruth Whitten described Mrs. Gomilla's store as a ladies' ready-to-wear store with a hat shop. She said Virginia Griffin ran it for Mrs. Gomilla. Margarette

Earle said the name of the store was the Style Shop until it moved across the street, then Snookie Anderson had the Tot Shop where the Style Shop had been. That move happened because Mrs. J. C. Temple bought the Style Shop from Mrs. Gomilla and changed the location.

John Webb and Nell Thomas both remembered Gandy's shoe shop. There was also a shoeshine chair which sat on the sidewalk in front of the store and had a steady stream of customers wanting their shoes shined. Edgar Norris worked at Gandy's when he was 12 or 13. He said they saved soles and heels of shoes and were busy all the time. There was also a television repair in the back.

Haskew Middleton also recalled that Rains Insurance was in the building and brought up a favorite memory of many. Atmore used to have a fire siren to summon volunteer firemen when a call came in. WATM radio would broadcast the location of the fire on "The Fire Reporter, Brought to You by W. R. Maxwell & Sons."

Ellie Bailey added that Ben Haley joined the business, and Helen Jones and Ruth Taylor worked there. Joe Maxwell was part of the group, entering in 1945 after World War II, and that was when "& Sons" was added to the name. Randolph Maxwell occasionally came home and had an office upstairs.

The history of the building goes back to 1918 when W. R. Maxwell and E. F. Goldsmith purchased it for an insurance company. Maxwell left the Bank of Atmore in 1931 and started insurance without Goldsmith. Real estate was added in the 1930s. Maxwell sold horses and mules

The Maxwell-Haley Building.

at one time and that brought joy to his sons because they had access to the horses which were kept at the house.

Some other businesses which were housed in the building were Will Hudson's clothing store, a hat shop, Securance Insurance group, New Dimensions Custom Picture Frames & Gifts, Glam Shak, and in 1990 Castleberry was added to the business name. The site was also the location of the old Magnolia Hotel which also served as a boarding house for workers at the Carney Mill. Presently the building is unoccupied.

The building is one-story, part brick, with a flat roof. Metal panels were added in the 1960s–'70s along with metal fixed storefront windows.

109 North Main Street
ATMORE OFFICE AND SCHOOL SUPPLY

Not much is known about this building. We do know that at one time the Bon Marche Dress Shop was located here and was run by Mrs. Paul Smith. Sye Morris and Sam Lazureth, who were Jewish, had a dry goods store. The major tenant was Atmore Office and School Supply, which Mac Mays ran for many years. It was probably constructed at the same time as 105 North Main Street because the styles are similar. There are inconsistencies in the building numbers, so one of the nearby buildings must have combined with another at some point. Jack Lufkin said that Mr. R. F. Cruit and Jack Curtis had Atmore Realty in the building at one time.

Mr. and Mrs. R. F. Cruit started Atmore Office and School Supply about 1940. The 1941 Atmore phone book lists the business as Cruit Office Supply Company. Mr. R. F. Cruit, manager. It advertised typewriters, carbon paper, salesbooks, and "anything needed for the office." In 1945, Mac Mays was principal at W. S. Neal in East Brewton. He moved to Atmore in 1946 and took over the business and added sporting goods. Having lots of contacts with many teachers, he knew he could sell to them. He retired and sold out in 1973 or 1974. Dee Peavy owned the actual building and the Cruits and Mays rented the space. Robert Maxwell said that at one time Dr. Peavy owned the building and G. A. Collins operated a general merchandise store. Helen Lumpkin said that Mary Peavy, Dr. Peavy's wife, and Virginia Griffin worked there when it was the Style Shop. Virginia bought her out and moved across the street to the building later occupied by Edgar's. It is still unoccupied.

Stylish dresses and school supplies sold at this location.

111 North Main Street
BRISTOW'S PHARMACY, BARNETT AND ASSOCIATES

John Webb said that W. R. Holley had the building first. Eventually Finklea Maxwell (brother of Willie Maxwell, the World War I pilot and namesake of Maxwell Air Force Base in Montgomery) had a pharmacy in the building. Claude Bristow purchased the pharmacy in December 1943, from Maxwell. Previously, Claude had worked at Escambia Drug Store with Winston Dunn. Bristow's was probably best known for its parched peanuts which were sold in the open door of the store. Evidence of how good they were rested in the peanut shells which littered the sidewalk. He also had the classic drug store round tables and metal chairs for patrons to sit at while they enjoyed their refreshments. Edgar Norris said he worked there from 1948 to 1950, parching and bagging peanuts. Lowell McGill said the store would open up all across the front and nature provided the air conditioning.

Bristow closed his store in 1975 and retired. Barnett and Associates, the Xerox sales agent, opened in the vacated space.

The building was noticeable for the 45 degree angle which recessed part of the building and made the sidewalk all the way to the railroad track wider than the northern part. It also has a brick cornice above a recessed brick panel on the front and side of the building. A date of 1910 was given for construction. I spoke with Beverly Bristow Lundberg about the flooring in the building, hoping that there were tile floors still intact. She replied that there were none there as long as she could remember. Perhaps the building was built too early to have them installed by the same person who must have done the others in town as evidenced by similar colors and designs.

Hot parched peanuts for sale here.

113 North Main Street
GREAT DAY DISCOUNT STORE

The 1972 Polk's city directory for Atmore lists this business with this address. The 1963–64 Polk's showed Royal Dollar Store here. Evidently, building numbers changed sometime because nothing else was ever mentioned at this address.

Once one of Atmore's Jewish-owned stores, which changed hands in an unusual way.

115 North Main Street
JASMINE PLACE, DANZIGER'S

This two-story building was constructed about 1905 and has a flat roof and projecting parapet. It is brick and poured concrete with a continuous slab foundation. There are three fixed windows, arched with stone sills. A 1940s wood shed-type awning with a series of Victorian era wood posts were originally present. The very decorative parapet cornice has sections of corbelling across the top and long horizontal recessed brick panels in the center of the facade below the cornice. It is flanked by recessed brick rectangular vents with vent holes. In the 1960s, aluminum and glass were added to the storefront. The balcony floor has four arched windows and a door which used to be a window. There is brick work at the top and a recessed sign area. The original design has changed considerably due to previous recent renovations. At one time, Dr. Holley owned the building and used it as a drug store according to John Webb. Mirtis Anderson said that it was Danziger's clothing store in the 1930s to early 1940s. The Simpsons also had a grocery store there.

Margarette Earle elaborated on the building's usage, saying that Tommy Stallworth had a salvage store and Dr. Mims had a dentist office upstairs. Frank Horne and Doug Webb, both lawyers, had their law offices upstairs. When they moved out, the building went to pot. Mrs. Earle got Dr. Holley to let them block the stairs and put windows in them. They put expensive items in the window. The building she is referring to is now 117 North

Main, a tiny and narrow space which also housed the early Albert's Cafe.

Jack Lufkin knew the building as Curtis Mercantile, one of the earliest stores in town. Charlie Moulton also lived upstairs. Dr. Zollie Mims had a dental office upstairs and a habit of throwing pulled teeth on the awning. Other occupants have been a dollar store, Your Little Pink Boutique, Farmhouse Antiques, Southern Charms and More, Designs on Living, Antiques and Other Fine Things, Michelle's Baking Company and Cafe, and Country Junction.

Jasmine Place, run by Frances Earle Dunn, served many Atmore women as the place for their bridal needs, whether it be bridal gown, bridesmaid's dresses, invitations, information on china and silver, or anything connected with weddings. High school girls filled the store at prom time, searching for the perfect evening dress to wear on that special night. An old 1951 picture, which appeared in 2004 in *atmore Magazine*, shows Bedsoles as occupying the building. The *Atmore Advance* has an advertisement in March 1933 for Danziger's. Old pictures and newspapers give clues to our town and have been valuable resources.

Helaine Danziger Birnberg said that her father was a merchant with a general merchandise store. It was the scene of many Sunday morning shopping sprees by prisoners from the state prison farm. Stores were not open on Sunday then, but since the Danzigers were Jewish, they would open up to help the prison out. The guard would call and ask if he could bring some newly released prisoners in to buy some clothes before they caught the L&N train out of town. Each man being released was given some money and a seersucker suit. The guard brought them to the store so they could get some khaki pants and a shirt and not look like a newly released inmate. The guard always stayed while the two to four prisoners were there to assure that Mr. Danziger was not afraid.

On June 4, 2007, Helaine came to Atmore to visit with me, and I asked her about early days in Atmore. At eighty-eight, Helaine was still spry and had a sharp mind. We spent hours with her regaling me with her life in Atmore from 1933 to shortly after the war when she married and left. What follows is part of that conversation which related to her father's store, Danziger's.

In 1933, Mose and Libby Danziger came to Atmore where they lived in a hotel for two weeks, then rented on South Main Street next to Dr. Holley and across from the Pattersons (where First Baptist parking lot is now). When setting up shop, they bought items from Alabama Dry Goods in Selma. The merchandise was aimed at white middle-class customers and high-class black ones. When you walked into the store, on the left side was a counter. Hanging from the ceiling were strings with ladies stockings which sold from 10 to 25 cents. Men's socks were also displayed that way. There was an island in the middle of the store with a big old-fashioned cash register. Around it was the place where packages were wrapped in brown, heavy paper, with string which was perched on a cone. The store sold only dresses, shoes, men's clothing, etc. Hats came stacked in big boxes.

The left side of the store also housed piece goods. Behind the counter, a case held thread along with bias tape and lace. The middle of the store had tables with men's and women's sweaters, overalls, jeans, work shirts, and Piedmont Arrow shirts. Those shirts had what was known as "aeroplane" collars which were made of the same material as airplane wings. These Piedmont Arrow shirts sold for $3.95, while regular shirts were $1.95. Mr. Danziger was proud to be the agency for them. The collars and cuffs usually wore out first on regular shirts. Shirts with the aeroplane collars could be reversed so they looked brand new. Her daddy sold so many of the more expensive shirts that Helaine said he could sell ice to an Eskimo. The right side of the store was dedicated to ladies' hats and men's items such as underwear, ties, caps, and shoes.

The last day of the store was an interesting story. About 10 one morning, a man came in and offered to buy the store. Mr. Danziger said everything was for sale except his wife and children. He set a price and the man agreed. The store was sold without taking any kind of inventory. The man went to the bank, got money, and brought it back. He paid Mr. Danziger in cash. Obviously, Mr. Danziger was shocked. He had a lawyer there at 3:30, took the man's money, handed him the key, and walked out. With no job and no money coming in, the family decided to move to Cleveland, Ohio, where they had family.

This is Atmore's skinniest building.

117 North Main Street
THE EATS SHOP, DISCOUNT TAX

Changes in street numbering occasionally occur and this seems to be an example. This minute building is across from the post office and squeezed between the old Jasmine Place and Earle's Jewelers. Catherine Albert said it was the first of the Albert family restaurants. Chuck Laue had a New York Life Insurance office there, and Linda Bumann had Linda's Lane which sold Avon and stationery. Discount Tax, Earle's Jewelry, and State Line Tax called the building home.

The Eats Shop is most remembered by our older citizens, many of whom ate there. It had a few bar stools

The Buildings

and three small tables along with a partition separating the kitchen. Dr. W. R. Holley owned the building. One day the cook left a pot on the kerosene stove while she went to get something from the grocery store. The pot caught fire, and the building was totally destroyed. Dr. Holley decided he did not want another restaurant in the building, and the Alberts were forced out of business.

James Forte added that there was a smokehouse in the back where Mr. Albert smoked meat and sausages. It stood until the rear parking lot was paved. Albert's served hamburgers, full meals, and beer. Clara Hodnette Foster of Montgomery said: "They had the best food in the world and lots of it. It was a small place, crowded all of the time, and everybody loved it." Joel Day loved to eat their beef stew and rice and got it every time he came to town. The cost was 25 cents a bowl. Margarette Earle said that at one time the building site was an open space and people would bring their mules and oxen from Main to Trammell through that opening. It's quite possible that the opening was caused by the fire at the Eats Shop.

The current building was constructed after the fire in the 1930s or 1940s. It is a one and a half-story building with a flat top and terra cotta coping. The exterior wall is brick veneer with stucco. It has one fixed wood window and a fixed metal awning. The building is only about six feet wide. There is a large rectangular sign panel above the storefront.

119 North Main Street
Earle's Jewelers, Southern Stems

Nell Thomas said she remembered when this business spot was occupied by Bubba Bowab. Others who have been here were Selma Bowab's dry goods store, the Economy Store, and Betty's Dress Shop. A Mr. Jackson had a discount drug store, and A. P. Webb Sr. and J. E. McCoy used it as a bank until the bank was built. The old vault was underground.

This 120-year-old building has a storied history.

The Earle's Jewelers building has a storied history. It was owned by J. F. Peavy and his first wife in the early 1900s. They sold it in 1906 to Mr. and Mrs. J. C. McCoy, who in turn deeded it to Mr. J. E. McCoy and Mr. A. P. Webb Sr. It ended up with Mr. and Mrs. J. S. Havard and passed to her seven children at her death. Finally, in 1973, the property was sold to Herman Earle.

Earle moved his business from right next door at 117 North Main. His first shop location in Atmore had been across the street on the north side parking lot of the post office. He worked with Dr. J. W. Stabler, an eye doctor from Mobile. The store sold eyeglasses, Christian books, and jewelry.

Frances and Wayne Dunn purchased the property and ran it as a jewelry store until about 2018. Southern Stems is currently located at the site.

The building is one and a half stories with terra cotta coping. In the 1970s, an aluminum and glass storefront was added. There is brick corbelling just under the roofline and recessed square vents with a round vent hole under the cornice at each edge of the building. The metal awning was added in the 1970s.

The original building dates to about 1904.

121 North Main Street
BANK OF ATMORE, BEN FRANKLIN, WISTERIA

The three most notable occupants of 121 North Main have been the Bank of Atmore, Ben Franklin, and the Wisteria. The building next door to the first Bank of Atmore became available, was purchased, and the contract for construction on the new building was set on January 3, 1921. The bank was to use the lower floor, with professional offices upstairs. The Post Office had space in the north end of the ground floor and the bank on the south end. Drs. A. P. Webb, Farish, McMurphy, and Nettles were on the second floor along with an attorney and the Atmore Public Library.[14]

Robert Maxwell said Randolph Maxwell had Atmore Finance Company upstairs in the late 1940s. Hugh Rozelle, Frank Horne, and Doug Webb had their law office there as well. James Forte said that Tommy Stallworth had

a store in the building when the bank purchased it and moved next door to Escambia Drug Store. Byard Swift gave a different location for Dr. Zollie Mims. Swift said the dentist had his office in the bank building and threw teeth out the window. Perhaps Mims moved and kept the same habit of throwing teeth.

Theodore Clayton opened Ben Franklin, an old-fashioned dime store. Another dime store was run by Ernest Jackson. Other tenants at different times were Atmore Carpet; Global Enterprise, run by the Dawe brothers; the Economy Store; Home Style Furniture; Sleepy Hollow Water Beds and Furniture; Randal's; Atmore Video; Lee's General Merchandise; the Wisteria, which was an event facility; Your Little Pink Boutique; Gladys and Dewey Johnson's clothing store; Oriental Trading; and Jitney Jungle.

The building was constructed around 1904 and was occupied by People's Mercantile Company. It is two stories with a flat roof with a stepped parapet on three sides and a stone cap. The facade was of continuous brick on a slab foundation. It had fixed double-hung windows. The iron awning and grillwork was added in 1997 or 1998. The balcony floor has double doors and three double windows, and a stepped roof. Downstairs are three triple windows, double doors, and double windows. John Webb remembered the original red tile canopy. Tile floors that followed the shape of the teller counter were probably removed when the building ceased to be a bank.

123 North Main Street
BANK OF ATMORE

This empty spot in the block has one claim to fame. It was the first location of the Bank of Atmore from 1904 to 1921. It was constructed as a one-story building with a flat roof and terra cotta coping. The cornice was a scallop pattern. Currently, the space is used as an alley to Trammell Street and for special events held downtown. The *Atmore Spectrum* of October 30, 1903, says of the new bank in Atmore, "The management will at an early date let contract for the building of a brick structure to be located between Curtis Mercantile Co. and L. Myer's store, which they hope to have ready for occupancy by Jan. 1st, 1904." W. T. Mayo of Pollard had the contract for building the structure.[15]

Lots of people remembered businesses they think were in the location. Annie Ruth Whitten mentioned Taylor Faircloth having a grocery store there as did Elise Crook. Margarette Earle recalled Massey Bradford with a grocery store that was sold to Grady Rhodes. Simpson's Grocery was also there. Gilmore Grocery, Louie Weeks grocery, and Jitney Jungle joined the ranks of grocery stores on that spot. The 1963–64 Polk's directory lists Carl's Decorating Services at this address. James Forte said the building burned and nothing was rebuilt.

A facade on an empty lot marks a former bank location.

125 North Main Street
BOWAB'S, THE NELSON PLACE

The earliest recorded deed which surfaced for this building was 1914. The one-story building has a flat roof with terra cotta coping. The exterior wall was stuccoed sometime in the 1970s. There is one off center entrance flanked by glass display areas. The bulkheads are covered with stucco. A metal awning, wood double doors, and painted tile and stucco are currently evident.

Bowab's was run by George and Blanche Bowab and was another nice ladies' ready-to-wear store. The layout of merchandise was similar to that of Danziger's and Carter's, with items on the sides and a central display area in the middle. Like the Cinderella Shoppe and The Greater Fair, they sold a complete line of Vanity Fair underwear and nightwear.

Other stores located in the building were Curtis Mercantile, Joyce's, Southern Addictions—Antiques and Consignment, Atmore Food Store, Jean Shop, and Junky Pearl—an upscale consignment boutique.

Unique to the store is that the whole building was air-conditioned in 1950. The store was sold to Bedsole's in 1969, which has resulted in many people saying it was original to the building but it was not. It is currently home to The Nelson Place, a Main Street event venue.

127–129 North Main Street
BENNESON'S DRY GOODS, BEDSOLE'S, WHISTLE STOP

Buildings have undergone change inside, outside, and with street numbers. Numbers 127 and 129 were at one time one store called Benneson's Dry Goods and then became Bedsole's, which expanded into 125. It is possible to still see where the doorways were cut into the walls to accomplish this. The result of this expansion is that 129 has now morphed into 127 and 129 being one

Above left, 125 had early air conditioning. Right, street numbers shifted over the years.

The Buildings

store. Unfortunately, no dates for all of this are available.

James Forte said that Theodore Clayton had a dime store before Bedsole's moved in. Mr. Forte had Forte's Discount Furniture there. The building was also home to Joyce's, Jitney Jungle, Annie's Community Cup, Simpson's Grocery, Irons Five and Dime, Sunny Skies (sewing operation), and American Tae Kwan Do studio.

The one-story building had terra cotta coping along the flat roof and stucco was applied to the facade in the 1940s. The storefront has two bays with two symmetrically placed recessed entrances with flanking display areas and a recessed panel area over each bay. At one time, the storefront was decorated with black and cream colored tile in a simple geometric pattern. There are decorative tile floors inside the two storefront doors.

The Whistle Stop Grill and the former Alabama Wing House were actually in buildings 127 and 129, but the address on the building is 129. The building is now vacant.

131–133 North Main Street
NEW YORK FASHIONS

This is another case of one building which used to be two converted into one with the street number of 133 North Main. The building has a flat roof with aluminum panels on the exterior walls. The building was completely remodeled to make it into one business. The bottom was tiled and stucco placed on top. There are three connecting large pane show windows plus another large window on the other side of the entrance door. Dress For Less occupied this building. It is now home to part of New York Fashions.

According to Thera McCoy, Foster McCoy, L. B. McCoy's brother, had a grocery store on the right side and a general merchandise on the left. Each building rented for seven dollars per month. This was during the Depression. John Webb remembered Massey Bradford's grocery store. Since the Webbs lived just up the street on North Main, his mother often had him running there for some necessary item. Nell Thomas remembered Fuller's Grocery Store in the same location

Edgar Norris remembered Carps Department Store in 131 and Lowell McGill recalled Olen's. It was also home to Diana Shop at one time. These two buildings were owned by Thera McCoy for many years. Also mentioned as being located here was No Returns and Alabama Aluminum and Vinyl Products. New York Fashions is currently located here and in building 135.

Left, two buildings converted into one, with one street number.

135 North Main Street

J&K VARIETY, LOOKING GOOD, WALLACE STORE

This building, which is a twin to 137 North Main Street, was built in either 1919 or 1920. It is believed that both buildings were owned by Ed and Comer Carter, with Ed and Zelma eventually having ownership of 135 that passed to their daughter Mary Carter Rabon. The building has a flat roof with a simple brick cornice. Aluminum siding has been placed on the storefront with the top part being removed in the 2010s to reveal the painted sign of J&K Variety Store. An aluminum and glass storefront was put on the building in the 1960s. It has a central recessed entrance, flanked by display windows. There are three sets of transoms with muntins. There are decorative medallions above and flanking the door and metal decorative posts at the corner of the bay.

Charles and Velma Bosenberg and Mildred Carter Dunaway said that Jimmy and Kathryn Long opened J&K Variety Store in either 1954 or 1955. This author fondly remembers attending the grand opening and the popcorn machine which was just inside the front door, right next to Granddaddy's store. The aroma of the hot popcorn was a beacon calling for my dime to purchase a bag of the hot heaven. Between the smells of Atmore Coffee Company roasting coffee beans and the popcorn machine at J&K producing fresh hot popcorn, the corner of Main and Ridgeley was a delight to the senses.

John Webb could add Wallace Store, featuring dry goods, to the list of tenants. James Forte recalled that Zelma Carter owned the building after her husband died in 1955, and Massey Bradford had a grocery store. Also present, according to Forte, was Sharpless Furniture, J&K, and Honey's which was run by Connie Diller. Joel Day reminisced about J&K, saying that his wife, Louise, went in to browse and look during her lunch break.

Lowell McGill and Mildred Dunaway talked about Teate's Grocery with Lowell remembering that he had a box which contained chocolate milk. Evidently, that was a rarity back then.

Other tenants which I discovered while researching were Kenwin's (which was present in 1964 and run by Norma Taylor), Looking Good Gifts and Accessories, Beauty Supply, Simpson's Grocery, Joe Albert's Grocery, Dress For Less, and New York Fashions.

The aroma of popcorn wafted from these doors.

137 North Main Street
C. K. CARTER

The building I was most excited about researching, which was mine at 137 North Main Street, has proved to be the most elusive with questions still not answered. I know that my grandfather and his family, Comer and Nancy Carter and three girls, moved from Repton in 1919. He left behind another brother, Charlie and his wife Daisy. Already in Atmore were brother Ed and his wife, Zelma Carter. What I can't figure out is why Ed and Comer paid Charles and Daisy Carter $2,100, which is shown in a document in the courthouse in Brewton and dated September 6, 1919, but not filed until April 28, 1923. How did Charles come to own the land, and when did he get it? I guess those answers are to be found in the graves of those concerned. I do know that Carter Brothers, as the store was known at the time, was first located across the street and moved to 137 when their building was completed. While doing research for his book on the history of the Bank of Atmore, my husband, Charles Karrick, was also looking out for information for me on downtown Atmore because I was compiling material for a future book. One of the things he found at the Archives in Montgomery was an advertisement in a January 1921, *Atmore Record* newspaper. The ad said, "We wish to announce to the public that we have moved to the corner building on Main Street across from the Curtis-Brooks grocery formerly known as the G. N. Harris old stand."[16] This tells us that the land was purchased in 1919 and the new building was built and occupied before early January of 1921. Thus, the 1920 date of when the store opened.

Frances Earle Dunn evidently gave someone at the *Atmore Advance* information for an article in 2019, which corroborates some of this information. "In 1920, Atmore had a lot of stables. On the corner of North Main was a big stable. They sold carriages prior to it being the Carter Building. It was a carriage stable where the chamber office is on the corner. Another stable was behind that."[17] If Frances's information is correct, that was probably the land she told me about in an interview on June 9, 2011. At that time, she said Atmore Warehouse Company deeded the land to Atmore Realty on April 26, 1918. This may be the land Charles Carter bought and later sold to his brothers Comer and Ed. We don't know who built the building.

The store was owned jointly with Ed working primarily with loans and Comer with retail. In 1932, Comer's oldest daughter, Mildred, married Bill Dunaway, and they worked in the store the remainder of the time it was open. Ed died in 1955 and his daughter Mary Carter Rabon still had Ed's part in the store until she sold out to Comer. Comer died in 1960 and Bill in 1961. Shortly afterward, the family closed the store but retained ownership of the building.

It was rented to Dewey and Gladys Johnson who had Johnson's Dry Goods. They had to move from their location in the Bank of Atmore Building because the bank was moving out to its new location on Nashville Avenue and

The Carter Building.

was selling the property. The Johnsons died in a house fire two years later. On February 1, 1965, the building was rented to I. G. Nichols, who opened and ran Nichols' Department Store until he retired on December 31, 1999.

Following the death of her mother and sister Mildred, Velma Bosenberg inherited the property. It was rented to United Bank for its Mortgage Services Division in August 2002. Upon Velma's death in 2006, the building passed to her daughter Nancy Bosenberg Karrick. She sold the building to Darcy Martin who opened an antique shop called Carter's Corner on December 2, 2014. After the antique store closed in November 2015, it became home for the Chamber of Commerce in January 2016.

Returning to interviews, Charles and Velma Bosenberg, as well as this author, remembered horse troughs and hitching posts on the Ridgeley side of the building. Velma went even further back to the 1920s with her memory of sleeping in one of the showcases and cutting her hand when she ran into one. We all remembered Mr. George Miller turning on the Christmas lights from a switch on a pole on the corner. John Webb and James Forte remembered a big horse trough in the middle of the street at the intersection of Main and Ridgeley. People would come north on Main and turn their horses, mules, or wagons around to head south. Farmers got water for their animals there. Webb said it was a brick or concrete trough and had permanent plumbing to keep it filled.

Nell Thomas recalled the Carter name was on the side of the store. (In later years, a Coca-Cola sign was painted on the side.) Nell said, "Mildred and Bill were so sweet to me as a little girl when I was playing behind the store."

Joel Day added more intrigue to the turn-around in the street when he commented, "There was a U-turn here (Main and Ridgeley) and at the Greater Fair in the middle of the road." Edgar Norris said the Carters had a potbelly stove to keep it warm. They had a door open to Ridgeley on the side. His mama sent him for sugar and flour, and he got gum as well.

The building, like its twin next door on the south, was built around 1918. It has a flat roof and a parapet with a limestone cap. It has a stepped parapet on the sides with a stone cap. There is decorative brickwork and a brick foundation. The original wood storefront and brick bulkheads are present. There is decorative brick under the roofline, including corbelling. There is a simple long, rectangular, recessed brick sign panel beneath the brickwork. Included are three sets of transoms with muntins and lovely decorative medallions and decorative metal posts at the door bay entrance. The exterior paint has been stripped to expose the original brick, and the vinyl over the transoms has been removed.

I gave Helaine space to describe the interior of Danziger's, so I would like to take equal space to describe the inside of C. K. Carter General Merchandise. This was a true general store which sold everything from farm implements and fertilizer to salt pork and hoop cheese along with clothes, fabric, and canned food items.

Upon entering the store, on the left side was a long showcase which held women's underwear, blouses, and sewing notions. Behind it was a short rack which was used to hang little girls' dresses. The rest of the south wall contained bolts of fabric, boxes of stockings, a Coats and Clark box for spools of thread, socks, and other clothing items. I always thought the stocking boxes looked so pretty, all neatly stacked on the shelf so the size and color could be read. I especially liked the color of the stockings named Red Fox. These stockings all had seams too. When a box was empty, I grabbed it for my paper dolls because it was the perfect size. The empty thread boxes were perfect to store my embroidery threads as well as my compass and protractor for math class.

Next to the counter was a higher showcase which was home to an adding machine and typewriter. It was on that typewriter that my uncle, Bill Dunaway, helped Calvin McGhee fill out some of the papers he used to get tribal recognition. Backed up to the side of that case was a stand for a large roll of paper and a place for twine, both of which were used to wrap up purchases. Paper sacks were only used for nails, candy, and a few other select items.

Further on back was a case for men's hats. My mother slept in that case as a small child when her parents had to work extra late. Another case held overalls. Continuing back were some farm implements and an old-fashioned but new wood-burning stove with lids which had handles so you could pick them up and fire up the stove. I often pretended it was my stove when I played house in my imagination. In front of it was a coal bucket filled with coal to put in the potbelly stove, which stood in the middle of the floor.

Near the front entrance on the right was every child's dream—the candy case. I was never told I could not have any candy, but I always asked first and ate very little of it. I guess that having the freedom to eat it takes away the desire. I would also go with Granddaddy to Mr. Alston's, right across Ridgeley, to resupply the candy case. Mr. Alston usually gave me a piece to suck on. Right behind the candy counter was the mirror to check out how a hat looked. The mirror was actually part of a beautiful piece of furniture. When the store was closing, my Aunt Zelma, Ed Carter's wife, and Mildred Dunaway both wanted the piece for their homes. They decided who would have it by a drawing and Mildred won. She used it in her hallway to put the telephone on, and it stayed there until the house was sold and I inherited it.

Beside the candy counter was the seating area for trying on shoes. If my memory is correct, there were two seats there as well as two stools for customers to put their feet on when being fitted. Shoes were in boxes on shelves along the north wall.

The big old cash register was about midway towards the back of the store, between clothing and food. It was one of those beautiful brass registers which weighs a ton. Along the wall were shelves with canned and boxed food. The only fresh food sold was hoop cheese, fresh fruit at Christmas, and salt pork which was in a large wooden box containing a deep layer of salt with a screen top to keep the flies out. A butcher knife permanently lived in the box and was used to cut the pork according to the buyers specifications. There was a counter for taking orders on which was a large scale. In front of the counter were kegs of nails, each size in its own keg. There were metal baskets of potatoes and onions which make perfect containers for potted plants today. It was with him sitting in a chair in front of these kegs, where I would sit on Calvin McGhee's knee and listen to him tell me stories. How I wish I could remember them today.

Right in front of the wide door which opened to Ridgeley Street were some chairs where my granddaddy "kept court." There were always men sitting there, talking with him. The colder it was, the closer to the stove they sat. The store was divided into a private area behind those chairs, but before you got there, pallets on the floor were stacked with bags of flour, meal, and sugar. These were in what were called "feed sacks" and ladies used the bags to make clothing. Some of the smaller bags had washcloths or cup towels sewn into the binding. Some even offered pieces of china with purchase. The back part of the building contained the safe and larger farm items which would take up too much room in the main store. I can remember horse collars hanging on the wall and plows on the floor underneath them. Fertilizer was also stacked up for sale. Back in the day, Uncle Ed would do his money loaning in that area. I always thought of it as dark because the light there was usually turned off, so I stayed toward the front.

The center section was filled with large wooden tables which ran parallel to Main Street. The very front table held bolts of fabric which sold at three yards for a dollar. On tables behind that one were oilcloth, men's shirts, blue jeans, dungarees, and work pants. There were probably five or six of those tables, and they went as far back as the cash register.

I received a good education in the store, learning math skills, measurement, handling and counting money, how to wrap packages, write receipts, and, maybe most importantly, how to be polite and treat all people nicely.

The author, with the sign from her family store.

The 'Holley Block'

William R. Holley graduated from Auburn and took up teaching as a career. He soon gave up teaching because of the low pay. He moved to Atmore and entered the drug business, owning Escambia Drug Store for many years. He sold the business at a profit and opened another drug store across the railroad on North Main Street. He found it confining and sold this business as well. He began to invest his money in farm land and city property. He erected a row of business houses in the northern part of town, which is known as the "Holley Block." Besides real estate, he also dealt in livestock and sold mules and horses. In 1932, he ran for mayor and served until 1940. The new post office, jail, and city hall were built during the time he was mayor.[32]

The Holleys lived at 300 South Main Street, and my grandparents lived catty-cornered behind them on Pensacola Avenue. A pathway was worn between the two houses where Ruth Holley and my grandmother, Nancy Carter, went back and forth visiting and having Coca-Colas. Also using the pathway were Dr. Holley and Comer Carter. However, more often than not, it was before sunrise when Holley would be coming over to join my granddaddy and maybe another man to go fishing. The backyard was lit up like a Christmas tree as the men loaded their fishing gear, bait, and food and drink into the boat. We all knew it would be fish for supper that night.

John Webb, who had probably lived in Atmore longer than any man I interviewed, had this to say about the Ridgeley Street area of town. Maybe you can picture some of these places in your head. "As a small child, Sharpless Furniture was on the corner of Main and Ridgeley. Behind that, Mr. Charlie Hall had a livery stable all the way to Trammell. Mr. Jake Merriwether Sr. ran a stable across the street. George Holmes opened a blacksmith shop. Q. E. Wells had pecans and agricultural products. He also had a steam cotton gin. Leslie McCoy had an electric gin and Currie's had a gin across on the left. Mr. Gainus had a tire shop. There was a livery stable on Ridgeley. Mr. Holley built a whole row of brick stores to rent out. Mr. Jim Fuller had a grocery store, J. B. Adams had Atmore Coffee, and a cafe was toward the end."

John would have been eighty-nine when I interviewed him, and he had a remarkable memory for his age. You can see from his description that the area north of C. K. Carter's store was mostly rural with cotton and mules until Dr. Holley came along and built his buildings.

The "Holley Block" as it appears today.

201 North Main Street, 100 West Ridgeley
TRADIN' POST, MCCOY'S SEED AND FEED, JUNKY PEARL

Entrances on two streets.

While this one-story brick building is on North Main Street, at one time it had an entrance on West Ridgeley, and there are quite a few businesses that had 100 West Ridgeley as their address. Others who were in part of this building were McCoy's Seed and Feed, Alton Tennant's Meat Market, a barber shop, Gandy Shoe Shop, and a fish market.

102 West Ridgeley Street
K&E PETS, FULLER'S GROCERY

K&E Pets was once housed in this building. Others mentioned by James Forte were a continuation of the Yellow Front, Jo Albert's grocery, Cecil Ellis's grocery, and Fuller's Grocery. James also added that R. L. Brown built the building in 1927 for $15,000 and he bought two of the buildings from Dr. Holley. From that statement, it stands to reason that Brown built some, or all, of the buildings in the Holley Block for Holley around 1927. He went on to say that Marvin King had Atmore Equipment in two of the buildings. He bought Rupert Watson's Farmall Tractors dealership and also had International Trucks and Buick and moved to a larger place on North Main Street. James said Holley had five buildings on Ridgeley Street. Judging from the small size of some of them today, they were probably built as larger buildings and divided at some time. Looking at the rooflines and design also supports this theory.

104 West Ridgeley Street
VIN-TIQUES

Emilie Mims had her stained glass shop here as well as Darryl Dawe's office. Wingard's Jewelry appears in the 1963–64 Polk's city directory as being located here. There was at least one other jewelry shop in one of the other Holley buildings so some confusion may appear. The 1988 city directory places Mims Stained Glass Studio here. Country Junction was also mentioned as a tenant. Nell Thomas said that her father had a meat market there—Tennant's Meat Market.

Thomas the Pig hangs from his tire swing at the entrance to welcome shoppers into Vin-Tiques. This combination of vintage and antiques makes an enjoyable shopping experience in Atmore.

106 West Ridgeley Street
RALPH'S BARBER SHOP

Ralph Odom was a long-time barber in Atmore who had a shop at 106. Sider's Shoe Repair was also in the building. Nell Thomas mentioned a pet shop and a cleaners.

The building was vacant in 2021.

Vin-tiques and an empty building are at the top of Ridgeley Street.

108 West Ridgeley Street
FORTE FURNITURE ANNEX, RALPH'S BARBER SHOP

Nell Thomas mentioned her mother's cafe here but failed to give its name. Forte Furniture Annex is listed in the 1988 Polk's directory. Someone also said they thought this was the building where a ceramic shop was located. Definite locations for these buildings are difficult to come by, so all listed may not be correct. Ralph's Barber Shop was also mentioned as being in this location. The building was vacant in 2021.

110 West Ridgeley Street
REYNOLDS' REAL ESTATE

Lisa Reynolds has painted this building a shade of light green with a white sign panel. It has seven transom windows above the recessed entrance. The colors make it cheery and inviting. At one time, there was an antique shop here and a City Cleaners. K9 Cleaners was also mentioned as was Mini Maids.

112 West Ridgeley Street
ATMORE COFFEE COMPANY

This building has also been freshly painted a cornflower blue with dark navy or black sign panels. A white metal awning hangs over the recessed entrance. The last six buildings on this street are all of the same design and were probably built at the same time and by the same person. The puzzle is that Dr. Holley only had five buildings built. There are six here now that look identical.

Skinner's Jewelry, Sutton's Music, Music Express, Roaster's Gallery, and the Coffee House, which opened in 2012, have all been accommodated in this building that the Atmore Coffee Company used from 1934 until the late 1970s.

Long gone are the days when I would stand outside my granddaddy's store at the corner of North Main and Ridgeley Street and sniff the pungent aroma of freshly roasted coffee. However, all it takes is a drive by a coffee shop and a quick sniff to bring those memories flooding back. There's just something about the smell of fresh coffee. There was a time in Atmore when that smell was commonplace and when almost everyone who drank coffee was familiar with Dixie Blend Coffee, roasted and sold by the Atmore Coffee Company

The coffee company also roasted peanuts for football games for many years. They would roast chestnuts at Christmas to sell, and most of those nuts came from trees at J. B. Adams's house and acreage on South Pressley Street, the present site of Adams Plaza. I remember munching on those warm peanuts as I sat in the stands of the old Byrne Field, wrapped up in a blanket with my feet in a paper bag to help them stay warm. Hot chocolate from a thermos helped too. Those were the good old days.

Floyd Adams's father, Herman, was the brother of J. B. Adams, and he had coffee routes each day of the week to surrounding towns and many country stores all over the area. He had a different route each day of the week. Floyd said he that when he was six or seven he would go with his dad during the summer. They would take along their rods and reels and stop and fish.

Slightly before and during World War II, most of the coffee came from Colombia, and it became much harder to get. The coffee routes stopped because gas and tires were rationed. The coffee truck continued to serve stores in Atmore, Flomaton, Canoe, Jay, and Brewton.

When the war ended, Larry Fischer, the nephew of J. B.'s wife, Josephine Adams, was hired to work at Atmore Coffee Company. Larry bought the business when J. B. retired. No one is quite sure when the store closed, but a newspaper article from 1977 shows him still in business. It probably closed about 1978 or 1979. I found a 1941 Atmore telephone directory where the store had a quarter-page ad and its phone number was listed as 85. In his 1943 master's thesis, "History of Atmore, Alabama and Surrounding Area," William Hugo Yancey devotes two sentences to the store. That is the only clue we have as to when the business was started. Quoting from that publication: "The Atmore Coffee Company established a

coffee roasting and blending plant in Atmore in 1936. In 1937 company figures showed 3,000 customers per week."

Cousin Carolyn Fischer Jenko, who lives in Kemah, Texas, wrote, "When Daddy moved from Booneville to Atmore, he moved in with his aunt and uncle, Josephine and Burl Adams. Uncle Burl owned the Atmore Coffee Company and Daddy worked with him there after coming home from the Army. He eventually bought the company. The main thing I remember was playing on the piles of sacks of green coffee when I was little. They were stacked taller than I was and fun to climb on. That, and weighing myself on the big scales."

Carolyn's brother, Lawrence Eugene "Gene" Fischer Jr., became interested in coin collecting. He would sort through the store's cash register, looking for unusual coins. Occasionally, he would find steel pennies, buffalo nickels, and mercury dimes. He once found a Silver Certificate among the bills. As they had been for Carolyn, the stacked burlap bags of coffee beans were the perfect place to climb and play on. The combined scent of burlap and coffee is one Gene has never forgotten.

Some paper bags came preprinted, but some did not. Gene recalls using a big ink stamp to print labels. Sometimes he was allowed to fill the bags to exactly one pound. They were sealed with a paper tape which was on a roller, and the tape was pulled across another roller that sat in water. The water activated the adhesive.

Gene's memories of riding with his father are eerily similar to Floyd's, even down to the towns they serviced. Gene said they would load the blue panel delivery truck with coffee and take it to restaurants and grocery stores in Brewton, Monroeville, Flomaton, Repton, Bay Minette, Huxford, Uriah, Frisco City, and all kinds of little country stores in between. He thought his father drank a cup of coffee at every restaurant he delivered to.[18]

Edgar Norris said he could smell the coffee when Larry was parching. He used old coffee croaker sacks when he delivered newspapers. Doc Sutton bought the building from Larry and used it as a warehouse. The roaster was left in the building. Doc sold the building to Tommy Gerlach for a restaurant which never happened, and he sold it to Robert Woods in 1997, who had it until 2007. Next, the building was sold to Joel Lambert, who brought the smell of roasting coffee back to downtown Atmore for a while.

Coffee once again reigns supreme in 112 West Ridgeley with the Coffee House serving up "espresso, smoothies, sandwiches, and other good stuff."

114 West Ridgeley Street
ALSTON WHOLESALE CANDY DISTRIBUTORS

My favorite store on Ridgeley Street was Theodore Shields Alston's Wholesale Distributors. He was the local candy wholesaler to stores in Atmore, and my granddaddy just happened to have a store complete with a candy counter. It was my treat to go to Mr. Alston's with him to get candy to refill the candy counter. I do remember being given candy to sample, and Granddaddy did sometimes let me pick out some different kind to sell, just to see if it was popular enough to permanently add to the store's merchandise. It was truly a child's paradise to be let loose in a candy shop. I don't remember it specifically, but I'm sure I got a piece of the candy to try once we got back to the store. It was a good lesson in business management for me. The 1949 *Atmorala* annual said of Alstons, "Wholesale Distributors—Candies, Notions, School Supplies." It still had an ad in the 1977 annual so was in business at least until the late 1970s.

Pullen's TV Repairs spilled over into this building and also 116. Until recently, when the building was painted a lovely shade of gray-brown, the Woodson's Furniture sign could still be seen on the recessed store panel. Thus, we know Woodson's would have been there at one time. Kudos for the owners of Cotton + Company for making the building so attractive for their ladies' clothing store. The wooden front doors are the icing on the cake.

116 West Ridgeley Street
PHILANTHROPIC SEED

Philanthropic Seed is another beautiful store on Ridgeley Street. The pale tan paint with black awnings is a perfect anchor store for the end of the block. Their painted logo on the side of the building is neat and appropriate. As their storefront says, "Happy—A gift you give for no particular reason but to make someone happy." This gift shop is a home goods store dedicated to brightening your home and sowing seeds of kindness and Jesus's love through monthly donations throughout the community of Atmore.

This location has previously been home to Lottie Tennant's Cafe, Forte Furniture, Woodson's Furniture, Pullen Metal Supply and TV repair, Bible studies, accessories, Mrs. D's Tax Service, Atmore All Star Cheer and Dance, Regina's Unlimited, and Forte Furniture Warehouse.

Left, Cotton + Company. Right, Philanthropic Seed.

111 West Ridgeley Street
COUNTRY CHARMS

The Country Charms building is one story brick with a flat roof and also a very high stepped parapet roof with central projections and brick cap. An off-centered and recessed entrance has aluminum and glass doors. Three large windows are to the left of the doors and a smaller window to the right. There are two entrances and an interior brick chimney on the side. The painted Escambia Farm Equipment sign at the top of the building is still visible.

The building was home to Escambia Farm Equipment for many years. One source says the building was built in 1946, and it is possible that Marvin King had his business, by the same name, in that location until he moved to north Main Street and Burton Stallworth took over. Helena Chemical Company was in 111 in 1989, but I'm not sure when they moved in or out. Country Charms was a gift shop located there until 2020, as well as R&J Wholesale Florist. Rising Stars Studio of Dance once occupied the building which is now for sale.

Below, former Escambia Farm Equipment store. Above right, former Forte Furniture.

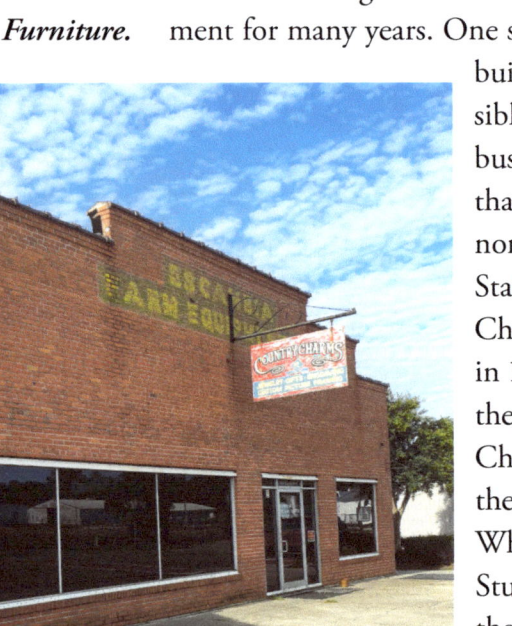

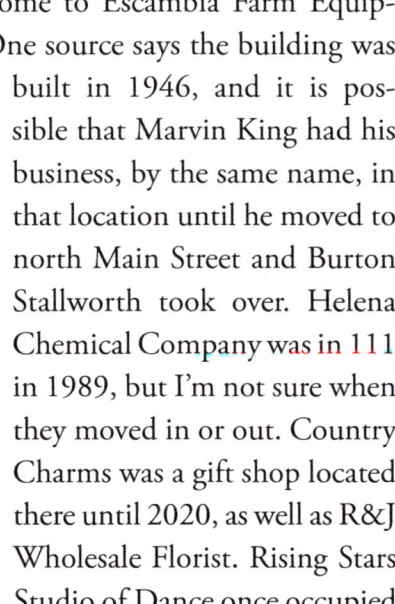

109 West Ridgeley Street
FORTE FURNITURE

This is a one-story brick building with a parapet and flat roof. The 1970s style storefront has aluminum and glass across the front, metal doors, and a metal awning. There is a wide limestone belt course beneath the roofline and above the storefront.

Surprisingly, when I talked with James Forte at length in July 2006, he really had nothing to say about his time in this building other than to state that his furniture store was located in it. I guess we had been talking so long that the poor man was tired and glad to be at the end of the last street.

107 West Ridgeley Street
ALABAMA ROASTERS

Currently, Alabama Roasters is in the building once occupied by the Anchor Cafe. The building and business are owned by Kerra Mascaro, who also owns the Coffee House which is just across the street. Coffee on Ridgeley Street seems to be here to stay, which is a good thing if you like freshly roasted coffee. J. B. Adams, with Larry Fischer later coming on board, were the first to roast coffee on Ridgeley. Joel Lambert followed Fischer, even being in the same building. He, in turn, has taught Mascaro, who is also in the Atmore Coffee Company building, the trick of the coffee bean roasting trade, and the smell of roasting coffee can again be enjoyed by downtown shoppers and businesses. It's an aroma everybody loves to inhale.

Going back with the history of the building, Jones True Value Hardware and The Sleep Shop, as well as the Anchor Cafe have been in this one-story, commercial building which is faced with vinyl siding. It has an aluminum and glass storefront and a flat roof.

105 West Ridgeley Street
PEACOCK'S ATMORE BARBER SHOP

This is a one-story, part brick building with a parapet roof, aluminum and glass storefront, and interesting floor tiles. Each tile design has a 1-inch square with 2x1-inch rectangles surrounding the center to form a 3-inch square block. Not an elaborate design but quite appropriate for a business. Claude Peacock had a barber shop here. Its name depended on the person telling the story. I heard Claude's Barber Shop, Peacock Barber Shop, Atmore Barber Shop, and Peacock's Atmore Barber Shop, but they were one and the same.

The building has also been occupied by A Cut Above, which was a beauty shop, Dugout, S&G Collectibles (baseball cards), Coiffures by Paula, and the Publican.

201 North Main Street
THE YELLOW FRONT STORE, JUNKY PEARL

You couldn't fail to see it as you were driving on North Main Street. The building was painted a bright, school-bus yellow, and stuck out like a bunch of bananas in a bin of dark purple eggplants. It was the Yellow Front Store, and yellow it was. The business was run by Ray Dauphin who sold groceries and a few other items. Before Yellow Front came along, there was Farmers' Supply. In 1923, Mr. Forte's father worked in a tin two-story building. O. H. Sharpless lived upstairs and had a furniture store down stairs. In 1926, a hurricane blew the top off, and the building was built back. He lost it during the Depression when the Bank of Atmore sold the mortgage to H. H. Dees. He and Roderick Faircloth put in Farmers' Supply which had general farming supplies such as feed, seed, and implements. Edgar Norris said that on Halloween boys from the high school would steal a wagon and put it on the high school porch. No one ever owned up, but everyone knew it was football players. This would have been in the late 1940s or early 1950s, Norris said. According to the 1941 Atmore phone book, Farmers' Supply also sold groceries, dry goods, and shoes. Their motto was "We go a long way to make friends." Additionally, they sold Armour and Merco fertilizer, seed potatoes, and Florence wagons.

In 1927, R. L. Brown built a building for Dr. Holley which included five buildings from the barber shop to the corner. This is the brick building which stands on the northwest corner of Main and Ridgeley and goes back down Ridgeley.

Cliff Frazier said that Jim Bell had a furniture store in the building, and Joel Day said the same, adding that he sold Fridigaire appliances. Edgar Norris remembered Clayton Hall selling antiques. Others in the location were Lee's David Discount Store, Darryl Dawe's office, Carol's Curiosity Shop, Bill's Dollar Store which opened in 1963, the Tradin' Post and Antiques and Collectibles. For a while, Joey Kelley was the owner, and Forte Furniture had a presence. Southern Social Boutique called it home and Junky Pearl is the current occupant.

This is a one-story brick part commercial block property with two bays and a flat roof with a concrete cap. Decorative brick panels are over the bay, and the foundation is brick. There is a shed awning with simple wood posts and a recessed brick sign area.

205 North Main Street
PEAVY-WEBB BUILDING

John Webb was the obvious one to talk about his father's old office, and he told a lot of history. When he saw a picture of the building, John's face lit up and he said, "That's Daddy's old office." He went on to say Dr. Webb came here in 1898, right out of medical school in Mobile. He practiced one year in Calvert in Washington County. Dr. J. F. Peavy had prescriptions in front and his office in the back. A mortar and pestle was on top of the gable in the front. The two men were originally the first doctors in Atmore. Dr. Peavy married Alice Carney and he built and lived in the Webb House.

When Webb heard Peavy was leaving, he came to Atmore and bought his home and office. Peavy later returned when his wife died and practiced here again. Webb married in 1898, but his wife only lived a few years. He had two children, Lizzie Lee and a boy who died. His mother eventually came from Texas to help with the children and had a boarding house in 1903. She taught, as John said, "the old lady" Sunday School class at First Baptist Church until she died.

The Peavy-Webb Building was built about 1897 and contained three rooms. It was later used as a photography studio, grocery store, telegraph, credit bureau, senior center, and Chamber of Commerce. It was moved to its present location on South Main Street by First National Bank, destroying its historical significance in downtown Atmore and proximity to the Webb home.

Jack Lufkin said the vacant lot on North Main Street between the Yellow Front and the Peavy-Webb Building was used for rummage sales every Saturday to raise money for the Methodists to pay the mortgage they owed on their church building. Indians sold patent medicine, which they said would cure any and everything. Ellie Bailey said the building was used as the post office for a year and a half while remodeling was going on at the post office. At various times, the building was a cafe, Hall's Tax Services, and the Credit Bureau of Escambia County.

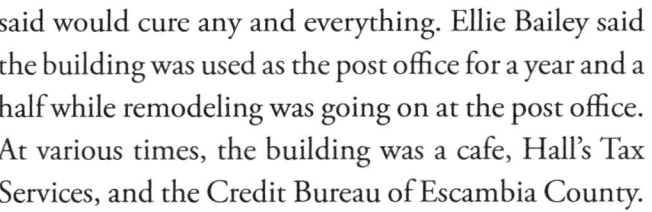

Above, the former Peavy-Webb medical office. Below, sometimes an empty lot is all that's left.

207 North Main Street
WEBB HOME

The Webb home was built by Mr. William Carney to entice Dr. Peavy to come to Atmore to serve as a doctor for his sawmill workers. He also promised to build him an office, which he did, right next door to his home. When Peavy and his family left to return to North Carolina, Webb purchased his office and house. John Webb said he was born in the house in 1919.

I asked Marcia Webb Pepperman to describe her grandparents' home, as I knew she lived in it for a while during junior high school: "It was a beautiful house surrounded by oak trees. There was a wide porch on the front that wrapped around to the south side and then a big porch on the back that wrapped around to the north. The windows along the house on the front porch came all the way down to the floor with shutters that could be closed at night. No air conditioning was ever needed in this house. The rooms downstairs were always cool with a nice breeze flowing from one side to the other. A long hallway divided the house with bedrooms on one side and a parlor, bedroom, dining room and kitchen on the other. Upstairs were several more bedrooms."[19]

Right, an old picture of the Webb home. Below, a branch of First National Bank is at the location now.

Ida Webb died in 1982, and her home sat empty for a few years until a decision was made to sell the property. The investors who bought the property had the house torn down and another Atmore landmark was lost.

206 North Main Street
WOODSON'S FURNITURE

Larry Fischer, Thera McCoy, Elise Crook, Bill Chapman, and everyone asked what was in that location answered "Woodson's." That could be because the name was on the building almost forever. Cliff Frazier said that Will Frazier built the furniture store for Claude Woodson, probably in the late 1930s because we know Woodson's was there before the war. James Forte gave a date of construction of between 1938 and 1940.

John Webb, who used to live across the street, commented that it used to be a vacant lot where a log track came through to get to Carney Mill. It was the neighborhood baseball field, and John played ball there. He knew it was vacant from 1929 to 1931, all the way to Ashley Street. Ashley was residential as was Main Street north of Ashley. Fred Curtis, Ted French, the Halls, Bowabs, and Mrs. Doty, mother of H. C. Williams, also lived in the area. Byard Swift added that Mariott Lufkin had a place on the corner of Ashley and Main where he hatched baby chicks.

The building has been occupied by Elite Sporting Goods, Alabama Archery Academy, Magnolia and Company, and U Financial, among others.

Memories come in strange forms, and that is true of some Emily Woodson Frank has of her parent's store. Emily said that as a girl in the 1950s, she remembered stepping into the brick storefront entrance to hide from a mean clown squirting her with a large fake baby bottle which was filled with water. She also recalled crying as she watched a man beat up and destroy old treadle sewing machines behind the Singer shop south of Woodson's. When she asked her father why the man was doing it, he said those sewing machines were built to last and the Singer people wanted to get rid of them and get them off the market so folks would buy the new ones instead. Emily also fondly remembered the old gas heater which stood at the back, blasting warmth into the showroom. Like I have items from my grandparent's store, Emily has some from Woodson's. She lovingly described the rolltop desk which was her father's and a very special turkey platter which was given to customers at Christmas.

204–202 North Main Street
WAREHOUSES

This building was used by many businesses as a warehouse for their extra goods. Included in that list are Farm Supply, Forte Furniture, Rupert Watson Hardware, Helton's, and Bateson's Furniture. James Forte said it was built for Farm Supply as a warehouse. John Shiver said H. H. Dees had it built and rented out the building. The small part (202) was added on for sewing and piece goods for use by Mrs. Dees. It was later opened to join Forte's. Forte said that Jim Bell had a used furniture store there and bought Sharpless Furniture out.

The building is one story with a shorter one-story wing (202) built of brick with a parapet flat roof. There is an earlier 1910s era parapet at the rear of the building, most likely remaining from an earlier building. There is one fixed wood window and poured concrete foundation. The main section has a central recessed bay flanked by wood windows. The shorter section has a central recessed entrance with original double doors and windows to one side. Concrete surround is all around the building and windows. An elaborate stepped free-standing parapet is behind this wing.

Part, or all of this building, has been used by Robinson Butane, which Root Lowery ran for his father-in-law with a name change to National Butane, later Florida Fabrics as noted in the 1972 *Atmorala*, then Joey's Furniture and Storage in 2000, and PCI Printing.

200 North Main Street
ALABAMA POWER COMPANY

It is not known exactly when this unique looking building was constructed, but the best guess dates it in the late 1910s or early 1920s. It is a one-story, freestanding, stucco commercial building with Spanish influences, including one decorative projecting parapet. It contains a simple parapet located on the rear facade with fixed metal windows and a poured concrete foundation. There are two irregular arched alcove entrances at the front corner, one on the front and one on the side, and a decorative sign panel is in the front gable. The front and side windows are the same squared arch. Stone sills are found throughout. The front parapet wall extends around the sides one bay deep. There is a concrete belt course near the roof all the way around the building. In the 1960s, an aluminum and glass side rear entrance was added.

The building started out as an ice house, and then Alabama Power moved in and was there for many years. The ice house was run by Mr. Ballard who lived on Horner Street, according to John Shiver. Others in the building have been Dr. Shackleford as an optometrist, Stephen Gross as another optometrist, Health Plus Chiropractic Center with Rodney Owens and Brannon Parmer, City Finance, Thompson's Home Furnishings, and Lone Wolf graphics.

126 North Main Street
WATSON HARDWARE

Byard Swift commented that Hillary Herbert (Hub) Dees said the lot was a mule barn when he came to town. I did some research to try and find out when this was and have two possible answers. Dees moved to Atmore in 1915 but left a year later, only to return permanently in 1924.[20] Knowing when other buildings were constructed in the area, I would say this one was probably built between 1915 but before 1924. That would be about right for a mule barn.

Bill Chapman bought the building from Ridgeley to the post office. When Long Motor Company closed, he leased the space to B. C. Moore, and the building in the alley was torn down for post office parking. Rupert Watson's father opened Watson Hardware, and Rupert joined up with Ace to make it Ace Hardware. Chapman opened Chapman's Ace Hardware in 1968 and closed it in 1997. Somewhere along the line, a pointed entry way was added to the front facade. I spoke with Bess Chapman Maxwell, and she said the change in doorway was done by Richard Maxwell when her father still had the store and was done to reduce the amount of glass windows across the front of the store. She also recounted that when B. C. Moore closed, an opening was cut through to the hardware and they used it for storage. That doorway appears to be totally opened up now.

Haskew Middleton and Lukie Anderson both said the building was Martin Automotive Company until about 1937 when Martin sold out to Rupert Watson. The 1951 Escambia County High School *Atmorala* said Watson Hardware was "The Right Place to Trade." Doris Landrum was a longtime employee. Lukie also said International Harvester, which was run by John King, was in the back of the building but did not say in what years. At one time, the building was owned by Joey Kelly and also housed overflow of New York Fashions.

Giving more credence to the turnarounds at the intersection of Main and Ridgeley and Main and Church streets is a comment Byard Swift made in July 2008. He said that senior girls rode down the street from Ridgeley to the Greater Fair (Church Street) then turned around and went back and forth. This was something H. H. Dees had told him. The girls were Margaret Sowell, Margarita Swift, and Elizabeth George.

The building is one story of brick and 1960s stucco. It has a flat asphalt roof with projecting pilasters and terra cotta coping. There was a gabled entrance portico with wood posts which changed the original facade. That gabled entrance has since been removed.

124 North Main Street
B. C. MOORE

James Forte and Byard Swift both recalled the creamery that Earl Goldsmith ran. Forte said Goldsmith manufactured the ice cream. Inside were a soda fountain and a lot of milk products. Mr. Goldsmith delivered ice and then

Watson Hardware, left, and Long Motor Company, right.

went to work at the post office. The creamery went out of business during the Great Depression. Forte Furniture opened up in June 1939. I remember Velma Carter Bosenberg telling me that right after she got married, her father, Comer Carter, went across the street to Forte's and bought her a wooden table and four chairs, saying she would need a table to eat on. I ate at that table as a child and am still using it and the chairs daily. As she and Daddy were fixing to leave town, Granddaddy rushed into his own store, cut off a piece of oilcloth, and gave it to Mother, saying she needed a tablecloth to go on the table.

Long Motor Company appears to have been the next tenant. Robert Long was a Plymouth and Dodge dealer. John Webb said that it was hard to get a car after the war. He said that: "Bob Long told me if I would take him, he could get a car. I did and he got a one-seat Dodge coupe with a bench seat. Three people could ride in it." Haskew Middleton said Long eventually bought out Hugo Esneul who sold Ford and began selling them exclusively. Joel Day recalled Chice Davis working there.

Long went out of the car business and sold the building to B. C. Moore, who did some major remodeling. Lowell McGill said Freddy Hobbs ran the store. Ellie Bailey said it was John Paul Jones. Could have been that one followed the other or one of the men could have been mistaken. Lowell also said that when Forte had his furniture store there someone came into the store, knocked him on the head, and robbed him. Edgar Norris said that Johnny Hoehn had a furniture store where the post office parking lot is now.

As time went on, West Brothers Clothing, Joey's Furniture, Fair Department Store, and J&D Discount City also had businesses there. New York Fashions continues to use the building as a storage facility.

The building is a one-story part commercial block which was completely refaced around 1970 with synthetic stucco. There is a flat roof with terra cotta coping. It was air-conditioned in the 1970s with glass storefronts installed as well.

122 North Main Street
ATMORE CARPET, ABC STORE, PFEIFER BAKERY

Enough people said Long Motor Company was in this building that it makes me wonder if 124 and 122 were open to each other at one time and later closed back up. John McKinley had the ABC Store at this location. James Forte said that at one time there was a meat market in a brick building where the parking lot is now. Helen Ramsey Lumpkin said Hugh Ramsey killed a bull and had it dressed there. She said Pfeifer Bakery was on the north side, which must have meant 122. She added that the bakery made Washington Pie in different flavors and that recycled bread was used in the pie in the early 1920s. I wondered what was so special about this particular pie that Helen remembered it 86 years later, so I did some research to find out about it.

The 1908 *Washington Post* said it is made of pie dough filled with stale bread, pieces of leftover cake, the refuse of the bakery, cheap spices, and a few raisins. It was a cake inside of a pie, very similar to the turduckens we have today.[21]

Martha Washington often served pies at Christmas called Washington Pies which included turkey, chicken, root vegetables, bacon, and herbs. Bread was what made the filling thick. It was covered with a top and bottom crust and baked. This was not a sweet pie but more like our pot pies and was served with gravy on top. I guess we will never know which one of the two Washington Pies Helen remembered. My guess is that it was the first one since Helen mentioned the bakery being at that location.

Bill Chapman said the building had a short-term dress store. Haskew Middleton said Robert Gordon and a man from Jay had a furniture store before Long Ford. They moved to Hainjie's building. Byard Swift and Lowell McGill remembered Johnny Hoehn having the Goodyear store and moving it to Nashville Avenue. He also had Hoehn's Trading Post. Mr. Jeter opened up Atmore Carpet which remains today.

The building is a one-story, part painted brick commercial building with a parapet flat roof that is stepped on one side. There are fixed aluminum square windows on the front and an aluminum off-center entrance. There are six garage openings on one side and a brick foundation.

114 North Main Street
US POST OFFICE, CARNEY LOGGING

The Atmore post office building really has little history because the same business has occupied the facility since it opened in 1936. However, before that time, Helen Lumpkin said the site was a logging place for Carney Mill Company. She said you could look behind and see the pond where logs were soaked. John Shiver said it was the Carney Mill Company engine repair shop and had double billboards in front to hide it.

My father, Charles Bosenberg, worked in the basement of the post office before the war when he was employed by Farm Security. Ellie Bailey also told of the time when the basement was a civil defense shelter (bomb shelter). He described the goods which were kept there and how H. C. Williams, the postmaster at the time, assigned each postal employee a job in case of an attack, his being Chief of Bunking. All of this took place back in 1961 during the Cuban Missile Crisis. Haskew Middleton also said the draft board was located in the post office as was an FBI office.

The outstanding feature of the post office is a mural which was done in 1938 by Anne Goldthwaite. During the Depression, President Franklin D. Roosevelt created the Works Progress Administration and hired artists to create original art works for public buildings in Alabama. Most of these artworks were murals which showed the local community, especially rural mail delivery. The one in Atmore is titled "The Letter Box" and shows a group of five children and an onlooker sitting with his dog, watching the children get a letter from their mailbox. It is indeed a lovely piece of artwork which adds life to the lobby of the post office. Goldthwaite's grandfather, George Goldthwaite, was a chief justice of the Alabama Supreme Court and was the first U.S. Senator elected from the South after Reconstruction.[22]

The building is one story with a basement. It has two octagonal bay windows with attached porch and a recessed entrance bay. It has fixed windows with stone sills and lintels. The front central bay is slightly extended and has metal scuppers and downspout. There is a stone belt course under the roofline. The building was built in 1935–1936.

112–110 North Main Street
HEAT SPORTS GRILL, 30 BELOW, EDGAR'S, CINDERELLA

While these are two distinctly separate buildings, for many years they operated as one, primarily when the Cinderella Shoppe and Edgar's were located there. The building was probably built around 1937, but it may have been later.

It is a one-story building with a flat roof. Weatherboard was put on the front facade sometime in the 1970s. There is a fixed window on the side with a transom running above it. Metal awnings were added when the building was remodeled in the 1970s along with siding. The outstanding features of 112 North Main are the green, cream, and tan tile floors at the door's entrance. Unfortunately, they were painted over several years ago so are no longer visible. An original door has been opened on the front.

Lukie Anderson told me that J. C. Temple built the building as the Style Shop, which was run by his wife. Clarence Thompson, a nephew of J. C. Temple, had a men's store on the north side of the building. Margarette Earle recounted that Mrs. Temple sold the business to Virginia Griffin, who named it the Cinderella Shoppe. Jack Lufkin said that Mr. Lufkin owned the building and sold it to the Griffins. The 1946 *Atmorala* said of the store in one of its ads, "It was exclusive but not expensive." Virginia Griffin, with Lillian Miller working with her, expanded the store into both buildings, according to Joel Day. The Cinderella Shoppe closed in 1974.

John Webb was the only one to give another earlier store in the building, and he said John's Cleaners was there and run by his wife, Mary Lynch.

Lucille King Swift and Francis Drew Smith were both living in Uriah and went to school together. Frances said they needed to move to Atmore and could get a job at the Cinderella two days a week. Lucille went and was hired for Friday and Saturday. She worked with Mary Bray and Ethel Grimsley Funk, whose brother had Grimsley's Department Store. Mrs. Autrey Graham did alterations at the Cinderella Shoppe and was the one to give Lucille the

Former Cinderella Shoppe and later Edgar's.

nickname of Lucy, coming from Lucille and Ethel working together like Lucy and Ethel on *I Love Lucy*.

Lucille said that when Ann Treherne was in college, she would model all of the clothes Mrs. Treherne chose to send to Ann at school. She commented that Mrs. Temple's Style Shop was across the street, and when Virginia Griffin bought it, she moved to the post office side.

For years, Billy Edgar ran Edgar's Business Machines on the south side of the building (110) and had Country Junction in the north side (112). The south side is currently home to 30 Below, an ice cream and sandwich shop. The Heat Sports Grill has opened as a restaurant in the north side. You're My Star Unique Boutique and Little Pink Boutique have also been in the building at 112 North Main Street.

108 North Main Street
H&R BLOCK

It is thought that the building was constructed in the 1930s and was completely remodeled in the 1970s. At that time, it was faced with vinyl siding It is a one-story building with a flat roof. In addition to the siding, an aluminum and glass storefront was added. At one time, the building was numbered 106, as documented by the 1941 Atmore phone book which listed Dr. Chapman's optician's office as 106. Sennie Chapman also had an apartment at 106. It has also been home to City Loan. Annie Ruth Whitten mentioned a Mr. Rosser as having an insurance office there. Drunetta Hammack said Ray Zwefield had State Farm Insurance and also a loan business. James Forte knew that it was used as city hall in 1939, and later, Dr. Farish was in one part and Dr. Chapman in the other, both working as optometrists. Joel Day said that Robert Maxwell was there for a while. H&R Block is the current resident.

104 North Main Street
ROBERT MAXWELL'S LAW OFFICE

Because of the confusion of 106 North Main Street, several people listed businesses at 104 which could have been in 106. If errors are made here, it is probably the numbering system which has people confused.

Going way back, John Webb said that Mr. Hilton had an office there. He was a businessman who owned a lot of property. Margarette Earle commented that Retha McNeely had a jewelry store in the building. Old pictures which have been in *atmore Magazine* substantiate this. Lowell McGill said that Mr. Manning had jewelry but did not know the store's name. There was also a Henry Lynch Jewelry Store before the McNeely's had their store.

Attorney Robert Maxwell's office.

One story about Dr. Chapman's tenure in either 104 or 106 was that he hired a black man with a mule and planted a garden behind the three buildings. He did this for ten or twelve years. Another piece of information which was shared is that construction was made of a one-story building in 1922 which was divided into three stores with Dr. Chapman having the middle one. Robert Maxwell's office building must have had a dividing wall at one time, which would have made the third store.

Currently, Otis Moore Law Firm, LLC and Shirley Darby's Law Office are in the building.

The building is a one-story commercial building redone in the 1960s. It was probably an older building but has been completely reframed with stucco and aluminum. It has a flat roof and concrete foundation. New brick was added over the stucco of 104, or else it was revealed when the metal was removed during remodeling in 2019.

102–100 North Main Street
LILES BUILDING

102 and 100 North Main Street are known as the Liles Building and were built at the same time by E. S. Liles in 1922. The building was constructed for Graham-Brooks to use as a warehouse. Brooks outgrew the building and built another on the corner of Nashville and Trammell streets. There were actually five buildings constructed at one time—the Liles Building and one behind it, two buildings in the law office next door, and the one which

houses H&R Block. This building is a two-story, flat-roofed building with a second-story balcony and fixed metal windows which were added in the 1990s. There was a recessed entrance into the first-floor business at one time.[23]

It is difficult to determine which businesses were in 102 and which were in 100 because the building is most often referred to as the Liles Building. Again, mistakes are probable as to the exact location of some.

We do know, according to Lukie Anderson, that Lorena Hadley's Beauty Shop was in 102 and that Jimmy Mason, who married Barbara Currie, had a restaurant in 100. John Webb said it was the City Cafe. Bud Mason had an "exclusive" restaurant. The spot was also used as a flower shop before it moved next to the funeral home. Earl Ethridge had a Carrier Air Conditioning business there as well.

Helen Lumpkin recalled John Stewart having a restaurant in 100. James Forte added that the post office was there for a few years before it moved into its new building in 1936. Haskew Middleton said that in 1948 Kimbrell Cunningham and his father had Cunningham and Sons State Farm Insurance. Jack Lufkin knew of Jake Curtis and Leon Brooks having a wholesale grocery upstairs. This eventually became Graham-Brooks.

Drunetta Hammack mentioned apartments upstairs. The longtime waitress at the Sweet Shop, Ophelia Hall, lived in one of the apartments and walked to work at the Sweet Shop every day. Edgar Norris remembered City

Furniture, where a "Dollar down and a dollar a week" was the slogan. Randolph Maxwell had a finance business. He also remembered the apartments upstairs and said his wife would get ladies from there and take them to church. Peacock Stationery and Storage was also in the building.

Other businesses mentioned were Mr. Esneul had car refrigeration and loans, Martin Weber a bookstore, H. B. Williamson an egg brokerage, a sewing mill where khaki pants and shirts were made during the Depression, News Room, Southern Computer, Southern Gold Buyers, Serenity Heart Home Health Care, Hair Creations, Healthy Minds Consulting, Superior Family Support Services, Zieback & Webb Timber Company, Peacock Photography, La Petite Maison Antiques, State Line Pawn Shop, Atmore Beauty Supply, Randolph Maxwell and Bob Long car loans, Lee's Music, Ayres Forestry, Kevin McKinley law office, Nichols and Cobb accounting office, American Red Cross, Ann Marie Nowak Confidential Counseling Services, and Transport Trucking. One of the most unusual stories about the building was that live chickens were thrown from the roof during the Depression.

101 East Louisville Avenue
RUFFLES BUTANE

This 1940s era building is built of yellow brick and is freestanding with a parapet front. The one-story building was remodeled in the 1970s and has an off-center, recessed entrance with brick surround at the recessed opening. There is a flat roof with coping.

Billy Watson, Rupert Watson's son, owned the building, according to Ellie Bailey. Billy had a loan office there and then sold the building to Billy Edgar, who used it as a warehouse for his business on North Main Street. Helen Lumpkin said the site was used by Carney Mill Company and logging by the railroad. James Forte, Cliff Frazier, and Byard Swift said that the *Atmore Advance* office was there at one time. Drunetta Hammack reported that Ruffles Butane was followed by Blossom Gas Company, and VW Finance was also at the site.

103 East Louisville Avenue
ABC STORE

This one-story brick, free-standing commercial building has a parapet, and flat roof with terra cotta coping. It was built in the 1930s. There is an original wood storefront and transom remaining, with much covered by brick during remodeling.

Everyone I questioned about the building immediately answered that it was the ABC liquor store, except for Edgar Norris. He recalled Northrup Seed being there at one time. He said they had a farm near Masland Carpet and raised plants for seeds. Those seeds were sold at this site. I have photos showing Mark's Barber Shop and Ann's Barber Shop at this location. It has also served as the County Food Stamp Office, County Welfare Department, Pension and Securities, Trimmerz Hair and Nails, and State Beverage Control. Tax Prep Evolution has also been here.

Left, Ruffles Butane; right, ABC Store building.

I have never been inside an ABC store but do have a funny story about them. When I moved to Atmore in the ninth grade, Rubye Lee Kizer was my civics teacher at Escambia County Junior High School. The class was discussing a topic where ABC stores kept coming up in the conversation. Finally, I raised my hand and, in all innocence, asked what an ABC store was? All I could think of was a store which sold alphabet blocks or other toys for small children learning the alphabet and wondered what that had to do with the topic of conversation in class. Before Mrs. Kizer could answer, the whole class, except for me, burst out laughing. It was a rather embarrassing moment for me, but patient Mrs. Kizer kindly explained that it stood for Alcoholic Beverage Control Board. I think she might have included that question on a test later in the semester. Oh well, in spite of being laughed at, I discovered what those stores were. Obviously, no one in my family used alcohol. The only bottle I have now is one I literally inherited when my grandmother died in 1990, and it has never been used—a bottle of crème de menthe to use in cooking.

105 East Louisville Avenue
MURRAY JOHNSON INSURANCE

The Murray Johnson Insurance building.

Not many businesses have called this building home. It was built in the 1930s and is a one-story, free-standing brick commercial building with a flat roof and terra cotta coping on three sides. The main entrance is centered on the large central bay and is flanked by large windows and sloped stone sills. There are also two secondary entrances to the right of the main one. There are metal casement windows throughout except for three small window openings with stone sills on the sides. There are recessed sign panels as well as a brick foundation.

Murray Johnson's Insurance was remembered by most people. Cliff Frazier said both the National Guard and the Chamber of Commerce met there when they were first organized. Haskew Middleton remembered the Food Stamp office and city restrooms. Several short-term businesses have been in and out very quickly.

107 East Louisville
CITY HALL

This building was the shining star of Atmore when it was constructed in 1936. It is a one-story brick, free-standing building with an Art Deco influence. There is a flat parapet roof, decorative brick pilasters along the front, and decorative brickwork beside the pilasters and corners. There are two decorative vents above the recessed front windows, arched double hung windows with wood surrounds throughout, and an arched entrance flanked by very narrow recessed rectangular bays. There are arched windows over the central recessed door with curved mullions in a fan shape. Sidebar windows are on either side of the door with decorative plasterwork on the facade in a contrasting white. It is on a poured concrete foundation. The building cost $10,000 to build in 1936.

John Shiver said that in 1936 or 1937, the agriculture class from the high school came to plant and landscape as a horticulture project. It was on Carney Mill property and had a pond which they kept logs in. That all had to be either filled in or drained to give usable land on which to build. Most of the older citizens I spoke with immediately connected it with City Hall.

Joel Day especially did since his wife, Louise, worked there. I well remember Louise being there because I went to City Hall every two weeks during my high school years to pick up my pay for working at the W. R. Holley Memorial Library, which was a city entity. Louise actually handed me the brown envelope with my cash salary in it. The money I made working at the library was all saved and totally paid for my tuition and room and board at Auburn.

Cliff Frazier said W. L. (Willie) Frazier built City Hall. Unfortunately, I neglected to either ask or write down his connection to this man. But an obituary lists his father as W. L. Frazier, so I suspect this was Cliff's father.

Also in the building were State Employment, Red Cross, G&R Satellite, Alabama Citizens for Life of Escambia County, and Atmore Civil Defense.

Besides City Hall, Nick Smith had Custom Travel here, and Nancy's Hair Salon and Nancy's Etc. have been located in the old city government building.

Watch Out for Trains

"Railroad crossing, look out for cars. Can you spell that without any R's?" How many of us asked that riddle as a child or would find ourselves saying it over and over as we waited at a train crossing for the train to go by? Brings back memories, doesn't it?

Atmore actually has two train crossings right in the middle of town. The Frisco crossing over Highway 31 is on a trestle so we don't have to stop when it comes through. However, the L&N runs right through town, parallel to 31 and crosses Highway 21, or Main Street.

The lonely train whistle at night and the rumbling of the cars as they race down the tracks can be heard blocks away. It is a soft, comforting sound during the night, letting us know that life and business goes on even as we sleep. Often I'll hear the whistle and then fall right back to sleep. It's just a part of nighttime.

Trains are quite loud for businesses in town. Conversation stops for a few seconds, then resumes. Either you are so used to hearing them that you totally ignore the noise, or you stop and look out the window to see what the train is pulling. Those whistles can be heard miles down the tracks as they approach crossings, and I often try to figure out where the train is and how long before it gets to downtown. The sound can be distorted and I'm rarely right in my estimate. But it's fun to try.

What do you do when you are in a car and are stopped at the crossing with the crossbars down, lights flashing, and bells dinging? Count the cars is probably the most usual answer. I've counted as high as 189, and that's a lot of cars. Some trains are so long that they even have another engine in the middle. Unfortunately, gone are the days when we could look for the caboose and wave to the conductor. And oh yes, remember as a child waving to the engineer who would almost always wave back?

I've seen some strange things come through Atmore on those tracks. Just the other day, a huge military convoy rumbled through, from large cannons, ambulances, tanks, to supply vehicles. And the Army went rolling along down the tracks.

Probably the most fun train I saw was as I was on

A landmark was lost in 1970 when the L&N depot was moved out of town. Its place was eventually filled by a smaller building used as a station for Amtrak during its short run through Atmore.

Highway 31, heading towards town and about at the satellite court house. It was going slowly, so I was able to drive past the entire Ringling Brothers Circus and see all of the circus wagons on the flatbed cars. Unlike the drab military convoy, these were brightly painted and decorated with advertising. It reminded me of the day Mother and Daddy took me to the tracks in Pensacola to watch the Ringling Brothers Circus arrive, except there the train stopped and we got to watch the unloading and parading to the circus grounds. It truly made an impression on this little girl. I enjoyed the circus that night too.

I remember another special occasion when the Amtrak Sunset Limited was going from Atmore to Mobile on its inaugural trip, and my parents were among a few lucky citizens who had been given tickets for the ride. I took them to town to board the train and watch it leave, only to have Daddy come out and ask if I'd like to go as well. A few people had not shown up, and there were some extra spaces. I jumped at the chance and hopped on for the ride, which was wonderful but way too short. It reminded me of the many times I had ridden the train from Pensacola to Atmore as a child and also riding the trains in Europe when we lived there. There's just something special about riding in a train. The view of downtown from a train takes on a whole different perspective too. It was lovely, and I was moving while the autos were stopped on both north and south sides of Main, maybe counting the cars!

Another memory is of a wooden bench on the grass on the northwest side of North Main Street, close to the tracks. Two or three farmers were normally sitting there, wearing dungarees and straw hats. It was just a place to sit and rest or chat with someone they saw in town.

My mother had a story about that bench of farmers, usually present on Saturdays when they were not working. Mother, her cousin Mary Carter Rabon and good friend Helaine Danziger Birnberg had been somewhere in Helaine's father's car, with Helaine driving. They got to the tracks and could see a train coming but knew they had plenty of time to cross. However, Helaine slowed because the crossing was rough. When she did, her car stopped, and she could not get it to move again. Of course, she was screaming, "What's Daddy going to do with me if I wreck his car?" In the meantime, the train was getting closer and closer, and its horn was louder and louder. The three girls were in panic mode with some choice things being said. Finally, Mother and Mary got out, but Helaine wouldn't give up trying to get the car going. Suddenly, the benchful of farmers appeared, picked the car up enough to free the wheel which had actually gotten caught in the track, and pushed the car out of the way of the oncoming train, just in the nick of time. Tragedy was averted, but all three girls were basket cases for a while. I just hope they remembered their manners and thanked the farmers who rescued them.

By the way, the answer to the riddle is "t-h-a-t," if you didn't know.

102 East Nashville Avenue
FIRST NATIONAL BANK BUILDING

Several of the businesses that were on the second floor of the old bank building had 102 addresses. As mentioned, under 101 South Main Street were Dr. Fosdick Crook's dental office, James McMurphy's law office, Dr. Julian Peavy's office, Atmore City Hall, and Hal Waller's office. Add to that Skipper-Phillips Insurance Agency as noted in the 1984 Atmore phone book and the USDA Farmers Home Administration.

Mid-century First National Bank building.

104 East Nashville Avenue
MCNEELY'S JEWELRY

Not much is known about previous occupants of this building, other than McNeely's Jewelry. Thera McCoy said that Retha McNeely was secretary to her husband, L. B. McCoy, and while there bought out a jewelry store in 1945. The store opened in a building on Main Street, and when the opportunity to move into a larger space appeared, the McNeelys jumped on it and moved into the 104 East Nashville location. The 1963 Polk's city directory lists the jewelry shop at 102 and OK Barber Shop at 104. Something is not right with the numbering of buildings and the number of buildings available. There were only two buildings between First National Bank and the pool halls, yet, 102, 104, and 106 all have businesses associated with them. One of these businesses must have closed or moved and when another moved in, the numbers were changed.

McNeely's was always a much sought-after place for local high school girls to find temporary employment during the Christmas vacation. Their aluminum foil-wrapped packages were prized gifts to receive.

When McNeely's closed, Herman Earle had asked for first refusal of the business, only to find out after the fact that it had been sold to Elam Fayard and would become Fayard's Jewelers with his wife, Sarah, in charge of the business. Main Street Jewelers eventually moved into the ground floor of the old bank building.

The McNeely building had its own distinctive style with an angled opening and large aluminum and glass, fixed metal storefront showcase windows.

106 East Nashville Avenue
STABLER'S SHOES

The 1941 Atmore Telephone Book lists the Electric Shoe Shop at this location. Their accompanying ad boasts, "Make your old shoes good as new. J. S. McGraw, proprietor—two doors from First National Bank." The 1963–64 and 1972 Polk's Atmore city directories list the store as the Electric Shoe Shop. By 1993, the phone book listed Stabler's Shoe Repair. Ellie Bailey also said Ebo Steele had a shoe repair shop at that location. It appears that the building had a long history of housing shoe repair stores, something which has almost disappeared from the scene in America. At least one of these shoe shops had a pool hall located in the rear of the store, according to Jack Beck.

All that was mentioned regarding the construction of this building is that it was built sometime in the 1920s and was a one-story building with a flat roof.

Below right, 104–106 East Nashville contained these now-demolished buildings. Bottom, a small park occupies the addresses today. The clock shown on page 100 stands to the left of the flagpole in the foreground.

108 East Nashville Avenue
POOL HALLS

Doug's Billiard Parlor and Stuart's Billiard Parlor were two of the pool halls mentioned as being at this location. However, most-often mentioned was the one run by Little John Harvey Stuart. It was a favorite hangout of the teen age boys, even though they were told by their parents not to frequent it. One said that they were better behaved in the pool hall than in school because none wanted to be kicked out of there. Evidently, they had a set of unspoken rules about what they could and could not do when inside the pool hall and everybody respected them. Ellie Bailey said you could get in trouble if you went in a pool hall because they sold beer. Not touching the beer must have been one of those unwritten and self-imposed rules. Unfortunately, Little John Harvey's pool hall caught fire and burned. Hours of playing pool and dominoes there were over, and the building was never rebuilt. Its empty space among the row of buildings was a visual reminder of a special place for many of Atmore's finest.

Jack Beck also related that the Atmore Dry Cleaners, operated by Russell Stilling, was also located at 108 East Nashville.

110 East Nashville Avenue
THOMPSON'S

James Forte went way back to when a store by the name of Greater Fair was at this location. It was run by Sam Morris and Cy Lazareth, a Jewish man. Agnes Smith worked there. The building later became Thompson's and was a clothing store. The 1972 Polk's city directory and 1993 Atmore phone book both show Thompson's Fine Fashions at this location.

Again, there is almost equal distribution on memories of where the Haberdashery was located. Some say here, while others said a little further east at 118 East Nashville. John Shiver said that Bill Brown, son of police chief Alfred Brown, had the Haberdashery and Zolan Middleton bought it. The site was later Thompson's. Byard Swift agreed. Lowell McGill added that George Scoggin ran Thompson's.

The building was first erected in the 1920s as two stories with a flat roof and simple cornices. It had a common bond exterior wall with stucco on one side and was on a brick foundation. The building was remodeled in the 1960s, especially the windows. Shutters and a colonial-style door and entrance were added.

Thompson's occupied this now-demolished building.

114–112 East Nashville Avenue
CLIFF BETHEA'S GROCERY

There seems to be confusion as to where Cliff Bethea had his grocery store, with almost equal numbers of people saying 118 and 114. With two entrances to 118, there is the possibility that there was a 116 in the western half of the building and that could have been where Bethea was located. It could also have been 114. Jack Beck, John Webb, Margarette Earle, Joel Day, Drunetta Hammack, Edgar Norris, and Ellie Bailey all gave this as the location for Bethea's Grocery. Haskew Middleton went on to say that Loree Jenkins and his wife took it over from Bethea as Jenkins Superette. The Superette is listed as being at 112 in the 1963–64 Polk's city directory. Drunetta Hammack said Mack Faircloth had a grocery store here.

The First Assembly of God had the building and used it for its youth activities. The Word of God Bookstore also called the building home as did Marie's Ceramics.

James Forte had a different story. He

Above, the now-demolished former Bethea's Grocery. Right, the clock that stands in the park where these buildings were.

said it was a two-story building with the Tradin' Post in a tin building. In 1923, O. H. Sharpless had a furniture store and lived upstairs. Russell Forte worked there and sold to Mr. Dees during the Depression for $4,000. James Forte bought it from Mr. H. H. Dees and sold it to Joey Kelly. The 1926 hurricane tore up the building, and it was built back as a brick building. The building description said it was built in the 1920s as a commercial style one-story with a flat roof and simple brick cornice. It had common bond walls and a brick foundation. In the 1960s, wood with aluminum and glass windows were put in the storefront. There were two entrances in the 1960s with two central separated pilasters.

118 East Nashville Avenue
HABERDASHERY

Carl Anderson spent quite a bit of time telling about his father's photo shop which was located in this building. Anderson's Photo Shop was in the front part of the shop. His mother, Snookie, would bring in clothes for the children to wear while having pictures made so that they would look nice, which would make the pictures turn out well and thus increase the money made. It was a good marketing strategy, especially for that period of time. In fact, it worked so well that she opened up her own shop, the Tot Shop, in the front of the store.

Edgar Norris said that Bill Brown owned the Haberdashery and Zolan Middleton and Cliff Frazier worked there. It sold nice clothes for men and boys. Another business mentioned by several people was Brislin's Cleaners. James Forte, Edgar Norris, and Jack Lufkin all mentioned Harry Brislin's business.

Nell Thomas commented on Cliff Bethea's Grocery Store. Ann Staff remarked that he wore a white apron and had a wonderful meat market. Jack Beck said A. T. Trimmer had Atmore Cafe here at one time. Also mentioned were Miracle Ear Hearing Aid Service, Beltone Hearing Aids, Mr. Barker's Grocery, and Brown Construction Company. As evidenced by the large sign in front in an early picture, Rent-to-Own was also there.

This building appears to have been built around the same time as the one to the east because they have the same style fronts and look connected. They may have been one large building or simply built at the same time by the same person and divided up into smaller spaces. It is a one-story, two bay, brick building with a flat roof and simple brick cornice. Two aluminum and glass storefronts with entrances and two brick pilasters are on the front.

Former site of the Tot Shop and Anderson's Photo Shop.

120 East Nashville Avenue
SAWDUST BOX

Because of the fire and rebuild next door to the west, it is impossible to know if some of the places mentioned above were at 122 E Nashville or actually at 120 East Nashville. Some are mentioned as being in both locations. The passage of time and fire damage have clouded memories to the point of not knowing which is true and which is not. Mrs. Grubbs's restaurant and hotel is one of those places. Haskew Middleton thinks it was at 120. He also remembered Boone's Cafe and Hall's Cafe being there; all three restaurants probably were in the same location, wherever that might have been. He did get it right with Dick Jones Framing, Edie's Craft Shop, and David Ragan with his framing.

John Shiver also had Miss Hattie Grubbs here. John Webb recalled Ab Lee with a parlor market (grocery market) and said that he was Son Horn's grandfather and Mrs. Rankin's father. Who your family was proved important to the older generations and helped make connections. Carl Anderson and Jack Beck remembered the Haberdashery and a pool hall. The 1963–64 Polk's Atmore city directory did list Bill's Billiard Parlor in this location at that date.

The building was built in the 1920s and was a one-story, rectangular building with a flat roof. It had a brick foundation. In the 1970s, fixed windows of aluminum and glass were put on the storefront. There were decorative brick panels and a series of cut out decorative squares all along the front fascia above the storefront, along with two recessed sign panels. The front was covered in red brick and sharply angled to form a recessed entrance bay.

The building was owned by Nancy Carter and Mildred Dunaway then, upon their deaths, by Velma Bosenberg who sold it in July 2000 to a couple from Kentucky.

The Buildings

122 East Nashville Avenue
BUS STATION

There were so many comments made by people about what was in this location that I decided to change formats here and list the people with their remembrances. None of this was in chronological order, and it would be nearly impossible to do so now.

John Webb—There was a brick building here with the Dixie Cafe on the corner. It had rooms to rent upstairs.

Nell Thomas—Goodyear Tire that Mr. Hoehn had. He was Ann Staff's daddy.

James Forte—Graham Oil Company. The front was cut off at an angle with gas pumps under a shed. Aunt Hattie Grubbs had a restaurant in a two-story building and rooms were upstairs.

Ann Hoehn Staff—There was a two-story brick building on the corner with lots of windows. Hoehn's Trading Center was here. Firestone Tire and Retread shop was in the back. John Hoehn first opened where Atmore Carpet is. Mr. Sutton had Sutton's Restaurant next door and Bill Brown had the Haberdashery.

Haskew Middleton—Sam's Place. Sam Byrne and Edgar Mason had a garage and parts. It was built as a silk mill in the Depression. The silk mill was later moved to North Main. Martin Auto Park and Chevy were sold to Gerlach. Johnny Hoehn had Firestone.

Mr. McCoy and T. A. Graham had Chevrolet here. Mr. Shiver's daddy had an automotive repair shop on the corner. There was a two-story building with rooms.

Byard Swift—Johnny Hoehn had Goodyear. Hattie Lee Hawke had Aunt Hattie's Restaurant. Byard went to Lions Club there.

Drunetta Hammack—Hoehn Appliance store. Bernard Trimmer and Marshall Nall worked for him. Mrs. Grubbs had a restaurant.

Joel Day—Red Vickrey's father had a filling station. Grimes Cafe, Hoehn's Trading Center, and Doc Sutton had several things.

Edgar Norris—The bus station was here. There was a two-story building. Hoehn's Trading Center burned in 1966. Mollie's mother worked there when it burned. TV and Recap and Goodyear managed by Mr. Stacey.

The 1941 Atmore phone book said of Grubbs' Cafe, "We are known far and wide for our chicken dinners." Rooms in connection. 24 hour service.

Also mentioned by others were Sutton's Restaurant, Happy Dayz Diner which opened in 2005, Rowlands Tire Center, and State Line Tires.

The original building was made of concrete with cinder block exterior walls. When it was redone after the fire, it has aluminum and glass windows on the storefront.

This was the long-time home of Atmore's bus station.

200 East Nashville Avenue
UNITED BANK

For all things historic about United Bank, I will defer to Charles Karrick's book *History of the Bank of Atmore*, which was published in 2004. In 1904, the first building for the Bank of Atmore was constructed on the west side of North Main Street between Curtis Mercantile Co. and L. Myer's store. The building was built by W. T. Mayo of Pollard.[24]

By 1920, space was becoming a problem at the bank and larger facilities were needed. The board of directors and stockholders approved to purchase the adjacent building from President McCoy and sell the current building to Thomas Alexander Graham. Wainwright Construction was hired to do the renovation on the new building. The lower floor was to be occupied by the Bank of Atmore and the upper floor made into offices. It was decided to allow the post office to occupy the north end and the bank the south end of the building.[25]

By the late 1950s, lack of space had again proved to be a problem. To understand how the bank ended up at its current location, Charles Karrick's narrative explains it in detail. The following paragraphs are in his words:

In 1913, Hotel Carney was sold to Dr. George C. Crook of Thomasville, Alabama. He moved to Atmore and operated it under the name of Crook Hotel. The hotel had 26 rooms, 20 baths, a large dining room, and sample rooms for use by traveling salesmen. In 1925, 18 more rooms with steam heat were added.

The Crook family operated the hotel until 1943. It later had two separate owners, M. R. Norman and his wife, Theodosia, and George Salley, and was known as the Norman Hotel.

Roy B. McNeely moved to Atmore in 1940. In 1946, he opened McNeely's Jewelry. In 1946, he established The Haberdashery, a men's store, which he later sold. In July 1950, he and his wife, Retha B. McNeely, bought the Norman Hotel, whose name he changed to Burton Hotel.

Many of us remember trips to the Burton Hotel as small children to have Olan Mills take our photographs. Joel Day was one who mentioned this as one of his experiences. I also remember getting all dressed up and walking into the hotel to have my pictures made. It was almost a rite of passage for Atmore's children. Margarette Earle said she and Herman used to go there for lunch.

At the March 17, 1958, board meeting, the directors agreed to purchase the Burton Hotel property on East Nashville Avenue, just south of the railroad depot, as a site for new banking facilities.

In May, 1958, the bank made a loan to director George Bowab and his wife, Blanche, in the amount of $51,500 which was secured by the Burton Hotel. The next month, the board authorized the bank to purchase "from Bowab for the same price" the Burton Hotel for a "future bank site."

On June 14, 1958, Mrs. McNeely sold the Burton Hotel to George Bowab, who sold it that same day to the Bank of Atmore.

At its September meeting, the board agreed to close the hotel as of the end of that month.

At the October board meeting, the directors approved the sale of the Burton Hotel to Mr. J. M. Bell of Atmore "with the understanding that the entire lot upon which the building now stands will be cleared to the ground level, and all debris will be removed, without unnecessary disturbance of trees and shrubbery, by April 10, 1959."[26]

Construction began on the new one-story building in 1960, and it was completed and opened for business on March 10, 1961. The building had approximately 5,000 square feet of working floor space. It had Atmore's first drive-up window.

In 1975, a second floor was added to the main office, the first floor was completely renovated, and a third drive-up window and a walk-up window were added.[27]

At the December, 1980, board meeting, a vote was taken to begin construction of a third story to the bank's main office building, plans which John Conn had drawn up back in 1959. Another major change to the bank building came in 1982 when a new sign was erected in front of the bank showing the name as United Bank.

In August and October 1995, two unwelcome ladies visited Atmore. Hurricanes Erin and Opal passed directly through the area, causing major damage. Erin devastated United Bank's main branch. The storm took the roof off the three-story building and water damaged all three floors. Bank operations were relocated in the bank warehouse and an office building behind the bank. While not realizing it at the time, Hurricane Erin was possibly one of the best things to happen to United Bank. It opened the door for new technology to be brought in and brought back the original teamwork and spirit of the bank.[28]

The bank building was a 1960s modern-style, reinforced concrete building with a flat roof. It had fixed metal windows throughout which were separated by concrete structures. The original facade of the building was totally changed with the addition of the second and then third stories.

This was the Crook Hotel, later the Burton Hotel, and finally the site of present-day United Bank.

101 South Main Street
OLD FIRST NATIONAL BANK

Little is known about the construction of the building, but we do know it was there in 1915 when a group of citizens met to form a new bank which became known as First National Bank. The first board of directors meeting was held in the office of Mr. C. C. Huxford, which was on the second floor of the building located at the corner of South Main Street and East Nashville Avenue.[29] It is a freestanding building, composed of two stories, with a flat roof. The walls are masonry on a poured concrete slab foundation. Remodeling was done in the 1960s. In 1970, First National Bank moved down Main Street to its present location.

Elise Crook said: "Fosdick worked upstairs. In addition to Dr. Crook's dental office, James McMurphy had his law office upstairs, along with Dr. Peavy in the back of the building." Mattie Lou Crook said Hal Waller had an office upstairs. Haskew Middleton mentioned McNeely's Jewelry in the building on the ground floor. Jack Lufkin said the Atmore City Hall was located on the second floor, over First National Bank for a period of time.

Edgar Norris recalled that Bobby Davis's parents had an accounting business upstairs. Main Street Jewelers took over after Fayard's Jewelers closed.

A picture of the corner of South Main and Nashville Avenue in 1949 shows a beautiful facade on the bank. A photo in the June 2002 issue of *atmore Magazine* on page 22 shows a picture of a parade on Main Street. The doorway to the bank had a gabled top with corbels supporting it. The beautiful brick of the building showed through, along with a belt course running under the second floor windows. I counted four windows on the ground floor of the South Main Street wall with a main entrance and a second entrance on the side. There are six windows showing on the second floor. The main entrance to upstairs offices faced Nashville Avenue.

At one time, there was a building next to the old First National Bank, which was run as Escambia Hardware. Mattie Lou Crook said it was operated by J. O. Lumpkin and Fred George. When First National Bank bought the building, Escambia Hardware moved into the building where Gilbert Barnett had his grocery store on Pensacola Avenue. Jack Lufkin said that G. R. Swift had money in the business. It appears that the store was founded in the early 1920s by Robert Cruit and H. W. Currie. A parking lot and drive through for the bank was built in the hardware space.

The original First National Bank anchors the left side of Main Street in this historical view.

I spoke with Jim Lumpkin, son of J. O. Lumpkin, and he said that his father, along with G. R. Swift and Fred George, owned Escambia Hardware. When Lumpkin died in 1962, First National bought the property and tore down the building for a drive-through. Randolph Maxwell was a partner with Lumpkin, and made arrangements to sell out to Lee Verne Seale and Mable Davis, who moved the business to Pensacola Avenue in the Barnett building. The original building was built in 1906, so it is distinctly possible that the business began before the 1920s.

Jim also told me about the George and Lumpkin Coal Company which operated out of the store. At the early times in Atmore's history, many buildings, including schools, were heated by coal, either in fireplaces, furnaces, or potbelly stoves. These two men supplied most of that coal. The L&N trains would get coal from Bessemer or Birmingham, bring it to Atmore, and leave the train car on a side track by the depot. A two-ton truck would be sent to the tracks, and hired men would shovel until the truck was full, take it to the coal yard, unload, return to the train track for more, and continue until the train car was empty. Large, empty, heavy-paper sugar sacks were bought from Pepsi-Cola Bottling Company and filled with coal. These fifty-pound bags were taken back to the hardware store. When someone wanted coal, they came to the store, went around to the back entrance of the warehouse, and it was loaded onto their truck or wagon. Jim spoke from experience as he helped fill the coal sacks and move them back to the store.

111 South Main Street
ABBIE STEWART HOUSE; FIRST NATIONAL BANK

In 1970, First National Bank moved into its new location at 111 South Main Street, the site of its previous drive-through building. This was a modern freestanding building with a flat roof. It had two stories and the front windows were covered in something dark which looked black from the road. A drive-through was attached to the back part of the side of the building. The building was covered with masonry and had fixed metal windows. In 2008, the building underwent a drastic renovation. The front now has the look and feel of a New Orleans-style building. Wrought iron balusters decorate the balconies on the north and west sides, and a gabled roof totally changes the roofline of the building.[30]

Several people mentioned the graves which used to be in the parking lot of First National Bank. Upon checking

1960s street view of Western Auto, City Cafe, and Escambia Hardware before demolition to build current First National Bank.

The Abbie Stewart House stood on the present site of First National Bank.

the story out, John Garrard said it was a fact. In fact, for years, a jar of dirt from the location was kept in the bank vault to preserve part of the old graveyard. John Webb said he and some of his friends used to play around the graves when he was visiting his grandmother. It is thought that the graves belonged to members of the Roberts family who had a house in that spot on Pensacola Avenue.

Before the first First National Bank was in the location, it was home to Abbie Stewart and her family. Marcia Webb Pepperman shared with me that Abbie and her husband, Jack, rented a house that stood at 103 North Main Street where Heavenly Escape Spa is now located and opened a millinery shop and boarding house. Later, she moved to a house at 108 South Main Street where Escambia Drug was located and continued her business. In 1901, she bought the lot where she built her home across the street from Atmore Hardware and kept boarders and made hats. The Stewart House was still there in 1957. Miss Ava Stewart, one of Abbie's daughters, was Velma Carter Bosenberg's second-grade teacher. Mother often told the story of Miss Ava being sick and how she went to her house to visit and ended up cutting out paper dolls with folded paper and making braided paper baskets. I remember seeing the house when I walked to town from my grandmother's. John Webb said his grandmother rented to Mrs. Tremmer, who had a beauty shop. Margarette Earle said that Dr. Goldsmith and Dr. Peavy had offices in a small wood house next to what was eventually the City Cafe. There was a little alley with grass and weeds between the office and City Cafe. Joel Day said that there were always people sitting on the Stewarts' front porch on Saturday, just people-watching and visiting.

119 South Main Street
CITY CAFE

Mattie Lou Crook said her husband, Wheeler, bought the building from Mr. Edwards from Flomaton. Wheeler owned Wheeler's Cafe when they married in 1940. He thought he would have to go in the service so he sold the business to Joe Holland, Lewis Shaver, and E. E. Manning. He later bought it back and changed it into a cafeteria. Haskew Middleton remembered Wheeler working at Sharpless' Sweet Shop across the street and then opening his own restaurant. James and Virginia Mills bought the restaurant in 1977 and ran it until 1982. John Webb said that there were no buildings behind the City Cafe building north of the railroad because the area was covered by Carney Mill's big pond. Unfortunately, he did not give dates for this fact. For a while, it was used as a warehouse for Western Auto.

If I didn't eat at home, I ate at Grandmother's because she always cooked a large midday dinner. Some of the girls in my class had to eat their noon meal somewhere else. The City Cafe was their preference. I went with them several times, and that is when I realized they served cafeteria style at lunch. When Mother and Daddy were building our house in 1961, we ate supper out almost every night because all Mother had to cook on was a hot plate, which was fine for breakfast. We all ate lunch at school and usually took a sandwich. That meant we ate our big meat at night. We would alternate between the City Cafe, Sweet Shop, and Albert's, as all had table service at night and we could get vegetables as well as meats. After almost a year, we knew the menus of all three quite well. In fact, the sweet waitress at the City Cafe would even tell us about things not on the menu that they could fix for us to give us some variety. If I'm not mistaken, our meals at all three restaurants cost about a dollar each.

The City Cafe was also the perfect place for a luncheon, bridal luncheon, or other special event, and many such events were recorded in the *Atmore Advance* social section.

Jack Beck mentioned Fred's Barber Shop with "Preacher" A. G. White and "Preacher" Peyton Taylor as barbers at a shop next to the City Cafe. He did not say whether it was on the north side or south side of the cafe.

The one-story brick building had a flat roof. It had 1960s style aluminum and glass storefront with two entry doors. The building was demolished in 2020 by First National Bank and is part of a park.

City Cafe, about 1940. Behind the counter are Grace Morgan, Wheeler Crook, and Mattie Lou Crook.

121 South Main Street
WESTERN AUTO

This building was also demolished in 2020, as was its neighbor on the north side. Records only say it was built in the 1920s or 1930s, so the date of construction is unclear. It was a one-story, square building with a flat roof. It had 1960s aluminum and glass windows and vinyl siding. Air conditioning was installed in the 1960s and that is when other remodeling was probably done as well. An aluminum awning was added, and two end brick projecting pilasters were present with brick panels in the front fascia.

James Forte said that Northrup Grocery was given to Henderson Northrup, who turned it into a Piggly Wiggly. Lewis Shaver bought it out as Piggly Wiggly. Mattie Lou Crook added that Voncile Northrup was a beauty operator and had a shop in the store. That shop evidently evolved into the barber shop that Haskew Middleton said was on the south side of the building. James Forte gave the name as Reid Barber Shop. Those could have been one and the same or each having their own shop at different times. Mattie Lou also said that Gail and Ruby Smith moved their Western Auto store to the building from the one they had across the street.

In more recent times, Edgar Norris said that Merrill Still bought Gail Smith out and had Atmore Appliances. Western Union also had a spot in the building.

125 South Main Street
ATMORE BAKERY

Left, as the building looked when occupied by Atmore Bakery, and, right, today.

The old Atmore Bakery building is one of the prettiest in town. The front is covered in brick with lovely diamond-shaped brickwork at the upper and left and right sides of the front. It's a very narrow building of only about 21 feet, but those feet hold some of the sweetest memories in Atmore.

In the March 8, 1934, issue of the *Atmore Advance*, there was the following notice: "G. F. Furney of Flomaton is moving his bakery from that city to Atmore and will be located in the Edwards Building on South Main Street. Mr. Furney formerly operated a bakery here in the same location." The business was started by Samuel Franklin Furney and Arabell Cain Furney in the 1920s or 1930s, thus giving an idea of when the building was constructed. Because of the decorative brick work, I would put it in the 1920s, based on other decorative work in town. Back in the 1930s and 1940s, cakes were not baked in metal pans like we use today. They were baked in wooden boxes made from soft poplar. When the boxes became worn, Carlton Sharpless, who worked for Samuel Furney from 1942 to 1944, would get shop students at the high school to build new boxes as a special project.

Mr. Samuel's son Lloyd (Sandy) and his wife, Cleo, and their son Lloyd F. Furney Jr. took over ownership of the bakery from his father. John Webb recounted that Sandy and Cleo Furney lived upstairs at his Grandma Stewart's house, just three doors up Main Street, and while they were there a baby was born. That baby was probably Lloyd Jr.

Smith's Bakery trucks worked out of the building in the back of the bakery. Local bread trucks met Smith trucks, unloaded and reloaded bread products, and made deliveries to local stores in the county. Virginia and James Mills purchased the bakery in 1972, as well as the City Cafe. They eventually moved the bakery into the cafe and had it until 1977. Jimmy Coker purchased the bakery building and combined it with Snyder-White Furniture. Merrill Still purchased it from Coker.

Betty Adams said, "When Larry Fischer was roasting coffee and Sandy Furney was baking, it made the whole town smell good." Not only did it smell good, it tasted good as well. Cleo would keep the bakery doors open while Lloyd was baking on days when Fall Festival was held on Main Street, and the odors coming out the door brought people in the door. Good marketing strategy.

Primrose, a children's clothing store, is located in the building today.

129 South Main Street
SNYDER-WHITE FURNITURE

Before Tommy White built the brick building which housed White Furniture, there was a small frame building on the corner. Mattie Lou Crook said that Mrs. Brantley had the phone company there: "Walter Scott Brantley had the first telephone exchange in Atmore in 1908. The exchange had a one-position magneto switchboard and was located in a small frame building at the corner of Main and Church streets, where it remained until 1947. Brantley died of a heart attack in 1934, and his wife, Sallie M. Brantley, and his daughter, Loutitia Cowart, continued to operate the business until December 31, 1942, when it was sold to Minor Corman."[31] John Webb said that three of H. C. Williams's cousins worked there: Maggie Gray; Jessie Bell; and Willodean Harper. Helen Lumpkin remembered the phone company being there in 1919.

Between the phone company and the bakery was a small open wooden building which housed a curb market, which was run by Charlie Steele and later by his son Claude. Wingard had a work table/jewelry store in one corner of the curb market according to Drunetta Hammack. The phone company was eventually moved to the next block of South Main. Northrup had a grocery store, followed by Lewis Shaver and Piggly Wiggly. Eventually, White built his building for White Furniture. Earl Snyder was an employee of the furniture store when White was killed in an airplane crash. Shortly after that, the store was renamed Snyder-White. Jimmy and Susie Coker had the business for a while. Bill Chapman said the Stills bought it after that and included the ambulance service with their appliances.

The building is rather nondescript and utilitarian with metal doors and windows, and it connects the bakery building on one side and the Church Street sidewalk on the other.

The business located there now is aptly named Williams Station Embroidery and Consignment.

201 South Main Street
GULF WINDS, BARNETT'S STANDARD, DEAN'S CHEVRON

The area where Gulf Winds now stands was once an open field. Lukie and Mirtis Anderson said they remembered when an open-air theater was there while the Strand Theatre was being redone after a fire demolished the old theatre. Haskew Middleton said the outdoor facility had wooden walls with no roof and wooden benches for patrons to sit on. Movies couldn't be shown until the sky was dark so shows were late starting in the summertime. This "open air" projection room caught fire while Frank Watson was the projection man. With a sawdust floor, he knew the trouble they were in and yelled to the people to get out. He jumped down from the projection room and escaped. Thankfully, no one was hurt. The movies were outdoors for about one year. Haskew would mow the yard and get a quarter for a ticket and an RC Cola. Haskew also said that he owned the area and when Standard built the station Ted French leased it. He was there for a year and then went broke. Ned Barnett took over. It was also Dean's Chevron Station before Gulf Winds built on the corner.

205 South Main Street
SOUTHLAND TELEPHONE

Atmore Telephone Company was purchased by Minor Corman in 1942 and moved to this location in 1947. The building was one the Corman family had constructed and it served them well until the company was moved a block east to Pensacola Avenue in 1960.

Others living on this portion of Main Street were:
207—Earl and Bertha Goldsmith and the American Red Cross office
209—Cleveland and Katie Pittman
211—Mrs. Grubbs
213—Ada Cruit; Elizabeth Grimes
301—House of Lowery Tourist Home, *Atmore Advance*
307— William and Ruth Holley

Floor tiles in the restored Tiger Lily shop, 101–103 North Main Street.

The Memories

Note: Memories of Raymond Barron, Ethel Lucas, Edith Mays, Ruthie Mae Rackard, Anna Bell Quarker, and Clint Turner were gathered in the spring of 2007 during interviews conducted by Nancy Karrick and Gloria Marshall Jones for the centennial of the City of Atmore that year and appeared in **Reflections: Conversations with Some of Atmore's Senior Citizens.**

RAYMOND BARRON

Raymond came to Atmore in 1919 as a ten-year-old boy. The trip was made partly by paddle wheel boat, and it took two days and nights to come from Marengo County. He remembered five stores when he came to Atmore: Carter's Store, Bowab's, Reid Drug, Carney Mill Company Commissary, and Grimsley's. Atmore even had an early taxi with Mr. Stone as the driver. The taxi consisted of two horses and a surrey. The area on the northwest corner of Main and Ridgeley was at one time a livery stable with horses and mules.

Trips into town were only on Saturday as he had to work the other days. Barron commented that he went to school barefooted, even in the winter. He went only through the fourth grade and then started working. At cotton picking time, the family would pick a bale a day. The gin they used was Robinson's and later on Currie's. For entertainment, there was always church on Sunday. This was a religious as well as a social occasion.

HELAINE DANZIGER BIRNBERG

Helaine moved to Atmore around 1932 and left after she married during the war. She lived in Texas most of the ensuing years but would come back to Atmore to visit and so never lost touch with her friends here. Her last trip to Atmore was to visit with this author in 2007, but I went to see her several times in Texas before she died in 2017 at the age of ninety-seven. Helaine was a born storyteller and could remember places and names better than anyone I know. Her stories were about the simple and commonplace things of her life, some of which I will share with you.

It was quite common for families in Atmore to have a washwoman who took care of the family laundry, usually at the washwoman's home. This person would come to the house, pick up the basket of dirty clothes, and then take them home to wash, line dry, and iron. In Helaine's case, this lady took the basket of clothes home to her yard where she had a big black pot full of boiling water on a wood and charcoal fire. She would literally boil the clothes, add soap and lye, and use a stick to move them around in the pot and get them from that pot to another which was filled with cold water. Clothes were rinsed several times, wrung out by hand, and hung on the line to dry. A long stick was placed under the line to raise it up so the drying clothes wouldn't touch the ground. Scrub boards were used on the really dirty laundry. Helaine said they smelled so good and fresh when the wind and sun dried and blew the clothes around. At the end of the afternoon, the clothes were taken down, rolled up, and put in the ice box. If they had dried out overnight, clothes were dampened again, starched, and ironed with flat irons. She noted that two irons were used, with one always on the stove heating while one was in use. "Those clothes were ironed picture perfect," Helaine said. Some were put on hangers and others were folded. All were put back either in or on top of the basket and brought back to the house, sometimes in a horse and buggy and later on in a truck. Interestingly, her mother never paid the washwoman. She was sent to the store in town, and Mr. Danziger paid the bill.

The teenagers loved to dance back then as they still do today, but their dances were quite different. Most were held in "juke joints." When I first heard Helaine use this term, I imagined a rather unsavory location. What a shock to find out that it was a filling station which had a few tables and chairs and a juke box. The teenagers would go in groups to these places and play the records and dance. She said that if a boy could buy a hot dog with sauerkraut and a Coke and put two or three nickels in the nickelodeon, they thought he must be deeply in love with them. What they didn't think about was that he had saved two or three weeks to be able to afford that date and the food.

Helaine talked about her high school days and of the football games held in the afternoon behind the school when everybody came to support the boys. She remembered Mr. Robert Hodnette and Miss Mary Hodnette and some of her other classes. Her comment about Home Ec was priceless. "In cooking, we made cream of tomato soup. It was nasty. Believe me, it was nasty." I can only imagine how bad it must have been.

Velma Carter Bosenberg

One evening during the aftermath of Hurricane Ivan, as we were sitting at the kitchen table and eating by candlelight, I asked my mother, Velma Bosenberg, to tell me about Christmas when she was little. She admitted that, at eighty-five years of age, she could not remember everything clearly. What she did remember is a special story about Christmas in the fairly early days of our town.

My grandparents moved to Atmore in 1919, and my

grandfather, Comer Carter, opened a general store with his brother, Ed Carter. Carter Brothers eventually became C. K. Carter General Merchandise and operated in the same location on Main Street for forty-two years. Those were the days when a water trough for the horses and hitching posts were located on the corner of Ridgeley and Main streets.

This is the story as Mother told it to me: Saturday nights and Christmas Eve were special nights at the store. Grandmother would bring her three girls along with Zelma Carter and her daughter, Mary, to town, and they would stay until the last wagon was loaded and the store could be closed. As the evening progressed, the young girls would become very tired. Grandmother and Aunt Zelma solved the problem nicely. They would make a pallet in the bottom of the large glass showcase out of the blankets which were sold in the store. The little girls would play quietly in the cabinet until they fell asleep. Grandmother was happy when they were asleep because they were out of her hair and she could devote her time to helping the many customers in the store. The sleeping children had to be carried out when the store finally closed.

This store was a real gem. It sold anything you could possibly want from a mule harness to shoes and clothing, nails, fabric, iron cook stoves, and groceries. At Christmas time, there were also some gift items and fresh fruit and candy. Many farmers would not come into town on Christmas Eve until after they had finished in the fields, cleaned up, and eaten. They arrived late and stayed late. There was lots of activity in all of the downtown stores.

December seemed colder then than now and none of the stores had anything resembling central heating. The family store had an old potbelly stove about two-thirds of the way from the front door to the back of the building. It was a gathering place as customers waited their turn to be waited upon. It also served as a place to visit with friends and neighbors and ask about each other's Christmas plans. Most of the farmers brought their children to town on that special night, and they would congregate around the coal-burning stove to keep toasty warm on one side and a little chilly on the other side. Many of the children would become sleepy, so their parents would take them to the wagon and bundle them up in the hay and cover them with blankets so the children could sleep while the parents finished their shopping.

Christmas dinner groceries would also be purchased that evening. Salt meat and sides of bacon were kept in a salt bin covered with a screen to keep the flies away. Farmers in overalls and their wives in calico dresses would select the can goods to go with the produce and meat they grew on their farm.

One particular customer always wore a bonnet that she had made. One day close to Christmas, she came into the store and took her bonnet off. She accused Granddaddy of taking the bonnet, and he had to pay her for it. Since she appeared with it on the next time she came in, he figured that she had really had it all the time. The tables were turned on her though when she wanted several items but could not pay for them. Always the gentleman, Granddaddy let her have the items, and the price she would have to pay was to quilt some fabric that he gave her. This quilt has eventually found its way into my home.

Mother said that as she entered her teenage years, she would take a break from helping the Christmas shoppers and go down to the drug store. Tony Albert was the soda jerk. She enjoyed sitting on the stools, sipping a drink, and talking. Years later, she acquired one of the metal ice cream containers from the drug store when it closed down its soda fountain.

Mother also related a story to me about Christmas and the store. There was one particular Christmas Eve when the store was especially late closing, and Mother and Daddy realized it was much too late to drive back to Pensacola. As always, they had thought ahead and were prepared, or almost so. She suddenly realized she had not brought a stocking for me to hang on the mantel. No need to worry. Granddaddy reached into one of the cases and pulled out a work sock (we call them monkey socks today), and I was all set. The sock was almost as big as I was, and it held oh so much. I still hang that same sock each Christmas, all these many years later, and it's even larger now because of stretching over time. Just another story of being able to find everything you needed in downtown Atmore, especially late on Christmas Eve.

From a small child who slept in the showcase until 1960, Mother spent almost every Christmas Eve in that store on Main Street. After she married and the war was over, she brought my father along to help. Years later, I was also added to the list of family members working there. It's hard for us to realize today how vibrant and lively downtown Atmore was on Christmas Eves of yesteryear. Those were indeed the good old days that memories were made of.

Linda Lumpkin Ellison

Linda and her family lived on South Main Street, and she was in a perfect position to know what was happening in town. Three things really stood out to her as far as memories of downtown—Christmas parades, the fair, and City Cafe.

Christmas was eagerly anticipated, and the Christmas parade was the event which started the season off. Linda remembers having professional floats and costumes for several years with local children riding on the floats. Fall was ushered in with football games and the fair, both held in the Byrne Field area of downtown. Even more special was the Friday designated as Fair Day, when students were given the day off from school to attend the fair. A tradition in the Lumpkin family was to go to the City Cafe for lunch on Sundays after church. Linda's favorite thing to get to eat was their fried chicken. I'm sure the Crooks would be pleased to know that Linda remembered their chicken after all these years.

Elementary school days at Rachel Patterson revolved around dancing around the May Pole, school plays with detailed costumes and music, school starting after Labor

Day when you started wearing dark cotton dresses with no white shoes or summer clothes, and fall and spring shopping trips to Mobile Gayfers and Hammels with lunch at Morrisons. Mardi Gras meant being out of school on Fat Tuesday and riding the Greyhound bus to Mobile and walking the streets, enjoying parades until the last parade of the day was over, then riding the bus home. She remembers having a new dress, slip, shoes, socks, hat, and gloves to wear to church on Easter, riding bicycles all over town and to swimming lessons at the old City Pool with its freezing water (it came from the ice house), and having to "save" the football coaches in life saving lessons.

There were birthday parties and summer dances at the City Park, AEA spring holidays at Gulf Shores at the Hangout, and polio vaccine on a sugar cube at the high school auditorium.

MARY AND GLENN JERNIGAN

Mary remembers downtown Atmore as being the place to be on Saturday because large crowds of people would come then. She would get to town early to find a choice parking spot and would sit on the car and "people watch." In front of the drug store was the best spot to park.

Glenn recalled that in 1949 Ford radically changed the body style of its vehicles and had a big parade to show them off. Pinkie Davis from Davisville had a Model T and led the parade.

The old Burton Hotel had an orchestra composed of Clint Hurd, Jimmy Eddins, Mary Nan Hurd, Eddie McNeely, and Glenn on drums. Eddie's family bought the Burton and lived there, and Glen would go and visit with him. He remembered other parades as well, especially the homecoming ones when cheerleaders rode the fire truck. Glenn's father worked at the fire station and drove the truck.

Boys will be boys, and evidently Glenn was one of the group. He recounted the skill some of them had in sticking straw covers on the ceiling of the drug store. Seems they put the paper straw cover in their chocolate milkshake and blew through the straw, towards the ceiling. They created their own stalactites hanging down from the ceiling. No comment was made about how they got them down!

NANCY BOSENBERG KARRICK

Memories. Oh, what special times our minds can recall. September is a real memory awakener with the first crisp hint of fall, the changing hues of leaves on the trees, the smell of burning leaves, goldenrod bursting with brilliant yellow color, and football season. It's the last item that has brought memories flooding back to me as the month of September dawned.

As a young child, I lived in Pensacola but spent many weekends and summers in Atmore with my grandparents and my aunt and uncle who lived with them. My parents were generous to allow me the time to spend in Atmore, where I learned to love the town and many of its people. On fall Friday afternoons, Mother would pick me up from school a few minutes early and take me to the Frisco train station in Pensacola. After buying my ticket, she would then put me on the train in the care of the conductor. I remember him coming down the aisle in his "conductor's suit," as I called his uniform, and punching my ticket with a hole punch. There was also the snack cart that rolled from car to car offering all sorts of tempting treats. It only took about two train trips before the conductor and I became quite friendly, and he took special care of me. It was a good thing, because I was only six years of age. When we reached Atmore, he helped me down the steps and handed my suitcase to my aunt, who was usually the one to come and meet the train. With a wave and "I'll see you next Friday," I was off to enjoy small town Alabama at its best—Football Friday Night.

Football season in the 1950s did not begin until the middle of September and went to about Thanksgiving. The weather was much cooler then than our August games and was downright frigid by the last game of the season. When I got to Grandmother's, I would immediately get out of my school dress and put on a pair of "pedal pushers," or slacks and a sweater. With this out of the way, I was free to head to the kitchen. Now, all of us know that the only time you can eat oysters is in a month which has an "r" in it. My whole family loved oysters and eagerly awaited September 1. Grandmother would be in the kitchen frying the oysters and French fries so that we could eat when the men got home after closing the store. The taste of those crisp oysters eaten in the breakfast room with the door and windows open to let in fresh air and the hum of the cotton gins will forever be etched in my mind.

Supper had to be eaten quickly so that we could make it to the game on time. Eight o'clock was the magical moment of kick-off, and we didn't want to be late. Ball games were played at Byrne Field in downtown Atmore, where the City Hall complex is now. Immediately adjacent to the football field was the fairground. In fact, the Utilities Board is still using one of the buildings that held the exhibits of the Ala-Flora Fair. More about the fair later.

The lights were blazing in the dark night sky as we climbed the steps to our reserved seats—yes, reserved seats. The center section of the grandstand was marked off in numbers, and you reserved the same seats year after year. I sat with my aunt and uncle, Mildred and Bill Dunaway, on the next to the top row. We were joined by Letha and Pellar Webb, Pearl and H. C. Williams, and Jimmy and Kathryn Long. My grandparents' seats were quite a bit lower down. I was never allowed to run along the sidelines as so many of the children did but rather was taught the rules of the game. I enjoyed learning the referee's hand signals and trying to figure out if the Blue Devils had made a first down.

I was always in awe of the cheerleaders who raised the American flag. The sound of the band playing the national anthem and watching Old Glory go up the flagpole were eagerly awaited each week. It was a time when baseball caps were not worn. Men wore hats, and no one had to ask them to remove them during the playing of The Star

Spangled Banner—it was automatic and done as a sign of respect for our country and its flag.

Then there were the cheerleaders. I guess every little girl dreams of being a cheerleader, Miss America, and a bride. For me, those eight girls were my heroines. I watched them practice all summer long in front of the high school and learned the cheers from listening and watching. On Friday nights, they looked so big and grown up in their circular blue skirts, lined with white on the underside and their white sweaters with the big blue "A" sewn to the front. Of course, there were saddle oxfords and bobby socks to complete the outfit. My favorite cheer was one that I named "the strut." The girls would form a long line and weave in and out of each other, making a huge turn at the end of the line before heading back in the other direction. What a gorgeous sight those blue skirts made when the girls twirled around. Of course, an added feature to the uniforms were the huge pom-pom mum corsages worn at Homecoming. No cheerleader would ever be caught without her lemons to suck on when her voice began to fade from the constant yelling.

So much for the high school girls. It was the boys we came to watch, and put on a show they did. Coach Floyd had his boys ready to play, and they were psyched up to win. Spirit was evident as they reacted on the sidelines and encouraged their teammates who were on the field. I'm sure Atmore didn't win every game, but they certainly gave it their all. As I mentioned earlier, it would get very cold toward the end of the season. The players were kept warm by wearing royal blue hooded capes. Jumping around a lot helped keep warm as well.

Halftime was always special because that was when I got a bag of peanuts to eat.

One of my uncles, Larry Fischer, had a coffee roasting company in Atmore. As a special favor, he would roast peanuts on Fridays to have for the game that night. Those little brown bags of peanuts were delicious to a starving child. Of course, the peanut hulls were fun to mash on the stands too. Not to mention, the fun of seeing the hulls go flying everywhere in the breeze. It was about this time that the thermoses of coffee and hot chocolate began to be opened. It was a veritable feast on that almost top row, with everyone sharing the goodies they had brought from home.

There were usually three bands that performed at halftime. The opponent's band would go first. At times, the L&N band would roll through first. Woe was the band that was on the field playing when the L&N decided to head down the tracks. Finally, it was time for the Blue Devil Band to take the field. The majorettes looked so pretty in their sparking uniforms, and everybody who was anybody was in the band. Their sound rang true in the clear fall night air, and their formations were done to perfection. If we were lucky, it was about this time that the big harvest moon would make its appearance, giving the evening a magical feel.

By this time, especially late in the season, the night air would be getting very chilly. Of course, the men all had on their hats, and many of the ladies had on scarves. Everyone wore gloves as well as coats. Feet were another problem, but that was easily solved by placing both feet into a brown paper bag. It made moving around a little difficult but kept the cold wind away from them. No one dared go to a game without the prescribed thermoses and an army blanket or quilt. We all bundled up, cuddled up, and enjoyed the game.

Earlier, I mentioned the fair which was held adjacent to the ball park. As much as I liked ball games, it was pure torture to sit in the stands and watch the fair in progress. The bright neon lights of the Ferris Wheel as it spun around and around, the sounds of the Merry-Go-Round, and the myriad of other sights made me want to be there, rather than where I was. My reward for being patient was a trip to the midway after the ballgame. However, my patience had to be further tested. Before I was allowed to ride on the rides, I had to go to the exhibit halls with the adults. There I rushed by the jams, jellies, needlework, flower arrangements, and animals, urging my family to move faster. Looking back, I realize how small that fair actually was compared to the ones in Mobile or Pensacola. But to a child, it was huge. The Tilt-A-Whirl was my favorite ride, and my dear uncle was the one who had to ride all of the rides with me. I also rode a horse on the Merry-Go-Round and squealed with delight when the Ferris Wheel stopped at the very top. From there, I could look back over the now empty Byrne Field and over much of downtown Atmore as well. It was a long walk back to the car, and I was one exhausted little girl. I can't remember anyone ever having to rock me to sleep at night. My problem was that I was so tired that I fell asleep before I could fully recount the afternoon and evening in my mind.

The rest of the weekend sped by, and before I knew it, I was back in Pensacola waiting for Friday to come so I could ride the train back to Atmore and go to another Blue Devil football game.

Because it was such a special time for me, I want to include some of the memories I have of Christmas in Atmore in the 1950s, when I was seeing it through a child's eyes. All of the magic and excitement was there along with something else I didn't recognize at the time, seeing how busy downtown Atmore was on this special night in December.

As I walked in some of the stores in Mobile and Pensacola in mid October, I complained to myself that merchants have pushed the Christmas season ahead again. How many of us remember the days when it was a cardinal sin to have any kind of Christmas decorations in the stores or at home until after Santa Claus arrived at the Macy's Thanksgiving Day Parade? Those were the days when Thanksgiving was a real holiday, not just a shopping excuse. Families gathered from far and wide to pause, share a meal, and thank God for the blessings they had received during the past year. While meal preparations were under way, the children excitedly watched the parade, smelled the turkey cooking, and waited for the grand finale—Santa Claus. It was then, and only then, that Bing Crosby's 45-rpm recording of "White Christmas" could be played. The Christmas season had arrived with all of its mystique, excitement, and secrets.

School children colored pages and pages of Santa, Christmas trees, reindeer, and bells, and hung them on bulletin boards or on the panes of glass in the schoolroom windows. We all made gifts for our mother and father as well as construction-paper Christmas cards for family members. Time was allowed to sing those carols and songs associated with the season. And, of course, we always had a Christmas play portraying the Nativity. How those times have changed.

Back at the mid century mark, Christmas celebrations in Atmore were very different from those of today. Everything was slower, even the speed limit. We took time to watch the grass grow and didn't complain about the train going down the track. Instead, we eagerly counted to see if there were over one hundred cars on the train.

Christmas decorations miraculously appeared in the downtown stores the day after Thanksgiving. They were not the elaborate bought decorations we see today, but rather, often a lit Santa face and cotton on the display window floor representing the snow that every child wished for on December 25. A few stores even sported a rare artificial tree, bedecked with fragile glass ornaments.

I was fortunate to experience the Christmas season as an "insider," meaning one who was connected with a store downtown. My grandfather had a general merchandise store, Carter's, at Main and Ridgeley, and I spent many a holiday season helping out. I began by wrapping packages for people who bought merchandise from the store. I still remember my aunt reminding me not to use so much ribbon so it would last the whole season. Stores were open on Thursday afternoon after Thanksgiving, so there were a few extra wrapping days added to December. I eventually progressed to the candy packaging. Boxes of loose candy, including those delicious chocolate drops and ribbon candy, were divided up and placed in cellophane bags and carefully weighed to be sure that the customer received his fair share. Nibbling was allowed, but, given the privilege, I rarely ate any. I'd much rather have a small sliver of cheese from the cheese hoop and a saltine cracker.

Five o'clock in the afternoon was a magical time for me as a child. I could go outside the store and stand by the light pole and watch the policeman come up and flip the switch to turn on the over-the-road Christmas lights. These were such simple lights, yet they delighted so many Atmoreans. Strings of colored lights zig-zagged across the street with an occasional red bell hanging from the string. What a delight to watch town take on an entirely different atmosphere once those lights were lit. Santa Claus could often be seen walking down the streets of town, talking to all of the children.

Christmas Eve was probably the busiest day of the year for shopkeepers. Many people would wait until that day to buy their entire list of Christmas presents. It was not unusual for the stores to stay open until midnight, or longer if someone wanted to purchase something. The popcorn machine at J&K Variety was kept plenty busy, as were the Bristows at the pharmacy with their parched peanuts.

Most children didn't get many toys throughout the year or fruit as often as we do today, and they were excited at the thought of receiving those items. The sidewalks were full of people milling about, shopping, and visiting with each other. It was just a very festive time. Granddaddy had large crates of apples and oranges positioned right at the front door so that everyone would know that he had some for sale. A popular item that has almost disappeared from sight today were the raisins still on their stems. It seemed as if everybody wanted some of them to go with their apples, oranges, and candy.

Exhaustion was the word as the store closed after a busy and hectic day. Maybe it was that exhaustion that caused a small child to vividly hear sleigh bells and to see Santa's sleigh on the way home. Looking back over more than almost seven decades, I wonder how my grandparents, parents, aunt and uncle managed to tend to the store all day, go home and get ready for Christmas morning, and then get up early enough to be sure the turkey was put in the oven. Granddaddy always shot his pistol in the air and cried out "Christmas Gift." Christmas had arrived—a time to celebrate with family, open presents, and remember the real meaning of the season, the birth of Jesus. In just a few days, the pine tree that we had so lovingly chopped down from the woods would be history, the house decorations packed up, and the countdown until Thanksgiving and the beginning of the Christmas season next year would begin.

Albert Spurgeon Kennington

Albert started his memories when he was about six, in 1948, and up to about 1960. The following paragraphs are his comments.

In these early years, my family and I went to town from the farm near Nokomis in a big farm truck. We owned no car then. My memory is that Daddy parked the truck on the SE corner of Trammell and Church—a vacant lot then—and we walked from there.

Let me begin with memories standing on the NW corner of Main and Church and tell you that I don't remember what was there then. A few years later, Henley and Agnes Smith opened The Greater Fair, and it was a lovely store. But in my early memory, they had a smaller store in the first block on Nashville Avenue between Main and Pensacola. They sold Buster Brown shoes, and Mama thought they were the best for me, although I also remember buying shoes at Anderson's.

Walking on Main Street on the west side, there are some stores I can't identify, and then there was Nall's Grocery. Without being sure of the order, there was the Sweet Shop Cafe, Atmore Hardware, Strand Theatre, Escambia Drug Store, Grimsley's and then Anderson's, both clothing department stores, and on the corner was wonderful Elmore's.

On the east side starting from Church Street was Steele's Curb Market and much later Snyder-White Furniture. Next was Western Auto and then the City Cafe. There was the old Stewart House where the bank is now. First National Bank was on the SE corner of Main and Nashville, with entrances on both streets. Much later, this became McNeely's Jewelry.

Before I cross the railroad, I'll describe a few other memories. Standing on the corner of the First National Bank and walking east, would be the OK Barber Shop, the Shoe Hospital, then a pool hall and Cliff Bethea's market. Next was the first store Henley and Agnes Smith had (it may have been called The Greater Fair), and on the corner of Nashville and Pensacola Avenue, there was Hoehn's Trading Center.

Going back to the corner of South Main and Church, and walking west on the south side of the street, was the American Legion Building on the corner, and in a ground floor room, there was the Atmore Public Library—a mecca of our every trip to town. Faircloth's Grocery was built, although the corner parking lot remained.

Across the railroad, beginning on the NW corner of Louisville and Main, there was Rex Sporting Goods and then Reid Drug Store. Next were a couple of stores or offices I can't name. There was Atmore Office and School Supply, Bristow's Pharmacy, and then in an order unsure to me was Earle's Jewelry, maybe the Ben Franklin store, Bank of Atmore, Bedsole's, Bowab's, Jitney Jungle was in there somewhere, and then C. K. Carter, your grandfather's store.

On the opposite side of this first block of North Main, beginning at Louisville, there are several businesses I did not and do not know. The first one I remember was Dr. Chapman, where I got my first glasses when I was in the fifth grade. Then there were others, and the Post Office and some more until Watson Hardware on the corner.

FLORENCE JONES KENNINGTON

(Albert Kennington: These are memories of Atmore told by my mother, Florence Jones Kennington, in a tape-recorded conversation with me in November 1996. She was nine years old when she moved from Sanford, Mississippi, to Atmore with her parents and younger brother in the winter of 1919. My grandfather, Jesse Albert Jones, was employed as the saw filer for Carney Mill Company. They moved into a house owned by the company on North Main Street. The memories which follow are scenes of her school days, 1919–1928. —)

There was a row of houses that belonged to the company, and our house was right where Gordon's Appliance Company was (304 North Main Street).

Our house was just a little, I guess you'd call it a bungalow. It was a four-room house. There were several that belonged to the company. They had picket fences around them and were stained brown. Some may have been stained a dark green with some white trim on them. They had bath rooms and a tiny back porch about six feet wide. Daddy had a little garden. The houses had electricity in them, and eventually we got a telephone, but not at first.

I don't think anything was paved. I remember streets in downtown Atmore being muddy. There may have been concrete sidewalks downtown, just for a block or two maybe, but I don't remember any paved streets. We lived in that house until 1928, right about Christmas time, when we moved to a farm Daddy bought west of town.

The grammar school was in the building that is now the educational building of the First United Methodist Church. It was an old red brick school. There was a wooden building with two classrooms in it between there and Horner Street. I believe the third and fourth grades were out there.

The Methodist Church was a white frame building on a lot sort of catty-cornered from there, on the corner of Horner Street and Pensacola Avenue.

After I got into the fourth grade, whenever the fire whistle blew was a very exciting thing. A siren would go off, and then it would go "woo-uh, woo-uh" and count off the different wards so that you would know where the fire was. McCoy Town was in Ward 4 (a name used years ago for an area on South Presley Street near Pine and Oak Streets). And the boy sitting right behind me lived in Ward 4. I remember one day we were sitting there listening to that, and everybody had their eyes on Murphy Ward. He was trying to be nonchalant about it, but we all wondered if Murphy's house was on fire. Hector Currie was the one who drove the fire truck, and he was our hero. There was nobody like him who got to drive the fire truck all the time.

I don't remember where the fire house was. City Hall was upstairs where First National Bank was, but I don't know where the fire truck was kept. The sawmill was on the north side of the railroad, in the area where City Hall is today. Later, Byrne Field was built on part of this site, and the annual fair was held nearby.

Some of the mill reached almost to the railroad tracks. I think the mill pond was closer to the corner of the railroad and Main Street. I don't know how big it was—maybe an acre—but there was a siding from the Carney Mill Company railroad track, on which a train could pull flat cars of logs beside the pond and roll them over into the pond. There were men out there, walking around on the logs with either pike poles or things with hooks. I think they were called Peavy hooks, to guide the logs around and feed them toward the mill.

Daddy was a Baptist, and I went with him to the Baptist Church. Once in a while I would go to the Methodist Church with one of my friends. The First Baptist Church was in the old building, the one on the corner of Horner and Main. Mama was a Methodist, but if she ever went to church, I don't remember. She was just so self-conscious about being deaf that she didn't like to go out in public. She didn't even like to go downtown shopping.

Carney Mill Company had a nice commissary. It was, for then, real modern. It was on the southwest corner of south Main Street and Nashville Avenue, right across from where First National Bank was. Mr. Grubbs ran it. I very well remember Mr. and Mrs. Grubbs. In the front of the store, there were glass show cases, and there were double doors. They had a nice ladies' ready-to-wear and men's ready-to-wear in the front part. Toward the back, there was a meat market. Somewhere back behind that there were offices, and they had a freight elevator. I think it must have been pulled with a rope, between the first floor and upstairs, where they moved merchandise up and down in the crates. There was a lady who was a milliner, and she made hats and sold ready-made hats on a sort of mezzanine floor. It was a very nice store.

Right next door to the Carney Mill company store was Benneson's. Bubber Benneson's father had a store, and there was a Bon Marche right there, too. Escambia Drug Store has always been in the same location, as far as I know. The pharmacist was "Doc," Mr. Holley. Grimsley's was on the other side of the drug store, then Atmore Hardware. And down on the corner was Lamont and Sowell's garage.

The next one across the street, going south, was the *Atmore Record,* the newspaper, and the jail was back there, a little old stone, concrete block jail. Dr. Mim's was the next place, and then the old Hampton House, a big old boarding house where we stayed for two or three weeks when we first went to Atmore. Across the street was Mayor Deese's house, then the big Patterson house, and then there was the Bennesons and the Goldsmiths, and then the First Baptist Church.

But back to school. The old high school burned down on New Year's Eve, 1924–1925. After the fire, while the new school was being built, classes were held in the Baptist and Methodist churches. Miss Mary Hodnette had her English classes over in the Methodist Church. I don't remember if there were any other classes there. I went to classes in both churches. The new school was finished by the following year, 1926. I graduated in the class of 1928 and there were twenty-eight of us in the class. Annie Ruth Holiday, Carolyn Long, Elizabeth Smith, Marvin Webb, Barbara Currie, and the Cunningham and Helton boys were some of my classmates.

A circus in town brought excitement. We were right there on Main Street where we could sit on our steps or hang on the front fence and see the whole parade—elephants, tigers, and all. Most of the time, it was up on the north end of Main Street, about where the water tank is now, and we were right there to see it all. We enjoyed that. Of course, we got to go to the show too.

Then, there was the Chautauqua. It came, more than once, and you could buy a ticket for the whole week. My girl friends and I would have a week's ticket to go every night. It was a really nice educational thing back then, and they had some good programs: musicians from European countries like Czechoslovakia and places like that. Some were politicians, I guess, but I remember way back then we were being warned about the Bolsheviks, the Russians, and about them taking over. They also had some programs that were very interesting to us younger people. We surely enjoyed it and always looked forward to it.

BONNIE BARTEL LATINO

My memories would be like most people who grew up in Atmore in the 1950s and '60s: movies at the Strand Theatre on South Main, especially for night and Sunday afternoon dates, and when we were younger, all day on Saturdays; Furney's Bakery across the street; and the City Cafe and The Sweet Shop, especially on Sundays for family lunch after church.

Of course, being on Main Street for Christmas parades, homecoming parades, and First Baptist Church Vacation Bible School parades with colorful crepe paper woven in the spokes of bicycle wheels, are standout memories. As an Episcopalian, I was also so sad we didn't have a parade!

One December, Pam Middleton and I convinced whomever was in charge of choosing the male clowns who, in complete makeup, crazy wigs, and costumes, walked along with the Christmas parade floats, to let us be clowns. No one suspected that we were teenage girls because it was just unheard of in those days. I think I was an ECHS senior and Pam a junior. We spent most of our time along the parade route hugging and giving big smooches to all the teachers watching the parade along Main Street. Oh! The giggles and gasps we heard that day. I don't remember ever revealing our identities.

One memory I may have that others might not is going downtown on local election nights for the results of the city council and mayoral races. Daddy was mayor pro tem for four terms (sixteen years), so every four years I went with him the night of the elections, after the polls closed. There was a huge white dry-erase board, always on Main Street in the block just north of the train tracks, and always on the west side of the street. Usually the board was placed somewhere between Rex Sporting Goods and Bristow's Pharmacy. In retrospect, I wonder why it wasn't in front of the small red brick City Hall, facing the railroad, and just around the corner. The old City Hall building is where Nancy's Beauty Salon is today.

But I digress. At intervals during the night as the collective votes from different areas of Atmore came in, a man, I have no memory of who he was, came outside and stood on an old gray, wooden ladder to write new tallies of votes. He used a thick black pen. In the earlier elections that I recall, I believe they used chalk on a black board. I'm sure there were cheers for all the candidates as their votes were added to the board. I, of course, remember best the loud cheers that always went up for Bill Bartel and his inevitable victories. I'm sure my mama must have gone, too, but I have no memory of her being there. Maybe wives and mothers stayed inside Reid Rexall Drugs at the soda fountain.

I also remember going to the Saturday movies with Jerrye Sue Forte as children, maybe ten or eleven, old enough back then to walk to and from South Carney Street to the movies on Main Street. There was a horror movie on. We got so scared that we squatted down on that sticky floor in front of our seats every time there was a real scary part.

One summer night I went to the movie with a

"sometimes" boyfriend. As we sat down, a classmate's kid brother in the row behind us pointed at me and yelled, "Hey! You were here last night! You've already seen this movie." I gave him a dirty look and said, "So what? So have you." My date then knew I'd been out with my other "sometimes" boyfriend. There were no secrets in Atmore, not even in the teenage dating world.

No memory about Main Street Atmore in the 1950s and '60s, and perhaps beyond, would be complete without mention of the enticing scent of parched peanuts, especially on Saturdays when Main Street Atmore became an audio gumbo of sounds from people, traffic, and the inevitable trains rumbling through our town—a town that wouldn't even be here if not for the railroad.

Ethel Lucas

Ethel said her family went to town one time a week, on Saturday. "That was when you went to town, on Saturday," she said. Her family always went by wagon, with the horse tied up by the depot. Since they raised much of their food, they didn't have to buy groceries, but they did buy some clothes and a few other things at the Carney Mill Store.

The Bank of Atmore was in its earliest location, near the former Earle's Jewelry, and the sidewalks were dirt. Ms. Lucas also recalled the streets being paved with bricks.

A log train came along Highway 31, and Ms. Lucas would watch them drop the logs from the train into the water at Carney Mill.

School for Ms. Lucas was Escambia County Training School. At one point, she had to walk five miles one way to get to school. I questioned her about cold and bad weather. "I didn't go to school when it was cold. If you want to go to school, go. If not, don't go. They didn't keep records back then and could pad the records if they wanted to. City children went to school more than those on the farms. Farm children worked. Only had three months of school anyway. Only had six rooms in the school building, with two grades in each room.

The fairgrounds were located in the area of city hall and the farmer's market. That was after the ponds were filled in with dirt. The Ferris Wheel was a special ride for children. There were special times when black people could ride the rides."

Helen Ramsey Lumpkin

Helen came to Atmore in 1919, when there were no paved streets. There was a sawmill and ponds in the area behind the post office. A large, two-story house belonging to Miss Ava Stewart sat on the lot now occupied by First National Bank and Trust. Mrs. A. P. Webb lived in the 200 block of North Main Street and Mary Nelson's house was next door. That house became Vaught Hospital. Mrs. Lumpkin remembered the Carter store as having everything in it—a true "country store."

Helen's family lived on a farm, and she had a pony cart with a rumble seat that she drove to school. The ponies were kept on the side street behind Alfa Insurance, and she walked the remaining block to school at the Methodist Church. One day, some children snuck off from school to play with the ponies. When they left the gate open, the ponies escaped and went home. Her father had to walk hers back to town so she could get home that afternoon.

Helen said she liked to play ball. In high school, she was on the girls basketball team for one year before Robert Hodnette stopped basketball because he thought it was not good for girls.

Helen worked as a beautician for sixty-eight years and started her career at the Carney Mill Company Commissary, going from selling dresses and groceries downstairs to upstairs at their beauty shop. She went to beautician school in Birmingham and said, "Back then, we had to have a chest x-ray and blood test every year." She noted that a white uniform and white shoes were mandatory because of state rules and slacks were not allowed. A permanent wave was $1.50, manicure 35 cents, and a haircut or wash and set was 75 cents.

BEVERLY BRISTOW LUNDBERG

I remember, as a little girl, on election night there was a huge board in front of Rex Sporting Goods with the candidate's names listed, and, as the results came in, someone would write in the new numbers. This board may have been on the back of a pickup truck. There were always lots of people gathered around visiting and waiting on the results. This was kind of a social event where all kinds of people, young and old, were gathered. It was an exciting time for all.

I remember when the cotton was being picked, the streets around Currie's Gin were lined with trucks and trailers packed with freshly picked cotton, waiting their turn for their cotton to be ginned. Daddy would take me over there, and the Curries would let me go in the gin and watch the cotton being ginned. It was amazing. The newspaper would always have an article about the farmer who had produced the first bale of cotton that season. That was a really big deal. There may have been a prize for that farmer.

I don't remember how old I was, but it was before the first grade, and I would go around the corner to Mr. Ray's Barber Shop (I think it was the Elite Barber Shop) and wait my turn to get my hair cut. While I waited, I would watch the barbers give haircuts and shaves. Before they would give a shave, they would pull this long leather strap out from the back arm of the barber's chair and sharpen the razor. The barbers would put really hot towels around the customer's face before the shave. There were always lots of bottles of good-smelling after shave and hair tonic. Mr. Ray would put this special padded board across the arms of the barber chair for me to sit on. He was always so kind, and I really liked listening to all the men tell jokes and stories or just talking about what was going on in town. Mr. Ray's wife later became my first-grade teacher.

I loved to watch the trains come through town. I would

stand in the door of the drug store and count the cars and sometimes there were more than a hundred. I always waited to see the caboose. Some of the passenger trains stopped at the train depot. It was fun to see the conductors taking up tickets and waving to people watching as the train went by. Once a freight train derailed right in the middle of town and spilled all its coal. It took a while for it to be cleaned up. I remember we had to go several blocks to a crossing to go home from the drug store. I also remember some people would put a penny on the train tracks and, after the train passed by, would find a flattened piece of copper. Everybody wanted one of those.

There were parking meters all along Main Street. You could park so many minutes for a penny and for a nickel you could park for an hour. Sometime customers would be in the drug store and see a policeman coming and run out to put more pennies in the meter.

Daddy bought the drug store from Mr. Finklea Maxwell in 1942 and retired in September 1975. At the time of his retirement, it was one of Atmore oldest businesses. It was named Bristow's Pharmacy. I loved going to the store with Daddy. I remember going by the ice house in the morning before going to open the store to buy a block of ice for the soda fountain. This was before ice machines. The drug store did not have air conditioning until late 1950s or early '60s and was cooled by ceiling fans. The front of the store had folding glass doors that allowed the entire front of the store to be opened to the street. Under the ceiling fans were four soda fountain tables and sixteen chairs where people would come and have ice cream or Coca-Cola and visit. Later a group of men around town would come in the mornings and have coffee, and as they say, "shoot the bull." Daddy would let me wait on customers and especially work behind the soda fountain. We sold ice cream cones. One scoop was five cents, and two scoops were ten cents. A small Coca-Cola was five cents, and large was ten cents. We also had milkshakes, cherry smashes, cherry cokes, vanilla cokes, lemonade, and limeade. Later Daddy started serving coffee. Daddy opened the store at 7 a.m. and closed at 6 p.m. Monday thru Friday. On Saturdays, he would open at 7 a.m. and be there until the last customer left, sometimes that was 11 or 12 at night. He would close Thursday afternoon, as did all the businesses in Atmore. Sunday, he opened from 8–11 a.m. and 2–5 p.m. On Sundays after church, we would go out to eat. One Sunday we would eat at the City Cafe, which was a cafeteria type line where Mrs. Wheeler Crook would always be there serving the best fried chicken. It had the best crust. The next Sunday we would eat at the Sweet Shop. Mrs. Sharpless would always have a piece of lemon ice box pie waiting for me. It had the best graham-cracker pie crust.

Back to the drug store. Daddy roasted the best peanuts in the world as far as I was concerned. He would always dip this big spoon in the roaster to get some out to taste to see if they were done. I liked them before they got real done. Daddy always knew just when to take them up. On Saturdays, he would start roasting the peanuts when he opened the store and continue until closing. Peanuts were ten cents a bag. I liked to bag them up so I could hold on to the top edges and flip the bags over and over to close the bag and then stack them in a wire basket in front of the peanut roaster until the basket was full. That took a while since they smelled so good. Everyone wanted a bag of hot peanuts.

One of my favorite times of the year was Valentine's, when Daddy would get in all the valentine candy. He had a huge display in the front of the store with all these beautiful satin cover heart shaped boxes. They had pretty bows and flowers. I spent many hours just looking at the boxes trying to decide which was the prettiest. After valentines, I would always get a box.

I have fond memories of being in the prescription room and watching Daddy fill prescriptions. I really liked seeing him compound the prescriptions using the mortar and pestle. He would make powder which he put in individual doses in a small piece of paper and fold to fit in a small cardboard box and then put a label with instructions. He would weigh the exact amount of ingredients on these really old scales that were enclosed in a glass box. He would also make up salves and put in jars. He always cleaned everything with alcohol.

When it rained a lot, Main Street would flood, and the water would come into all the stores. We would get big brooms and sweep and sweep to try to keep the water out. I remember one night the police called about the water in the stores, and Mama and Daddy and I went to the store and started sweeping. There were several cardboard displays that were beginning to tip over due to the water. We were able to get the merchandise off before they fell. When cars would come down the street, the water would come in more.

Back in the 1950s, Saturday Atmore was booming. Everybody came to town on Saturday and would stay and shop all day into the night. Most of the farmers and family would kind of dress up to come to town. They had a television in the window of one of the stores down from Long Motor Company and lots of people would stand or sit on the hoods of their parked cars and watch the Saturday night fights. I was just fascinated by a TV.

I remember the football stadium was one block east of Main Street. People would park all up and down Main Street and walk through the Post Office driveway to the stadium.

One of my favorite things to do was go next door to the Ben Franklin five and dime store and just look around until I found something I thought I just had to have, then go ask Mama or Daddy for some money to buy it. I don't think I got the money very often so I would forget about it and go back another day and find something else.

During the summer, most of the children went barefooted downtown, and our feet would be black with dirt. Daddy would scrub my feet with Lava soap.

I remember the scales on the sidewalk. Daddy had one outside the front of the store, and there was one in front of Reid Drug Store. You would step up on the scales and put a penny in the slot to get your weight and your fortune. It was more fun to read your fortune than your weight.

When I was in the sixth grade, Ann McKinley and I would go to Helen Lumpkin's beauty parlor on Nashville Avenue to get manicures. Mrs. Lumpkin would use broken pieces of a light bulb that she had smoothed out to push back our cuticles after she had filed and soaked our nails. That always felt so good. Then she would put some light pink polish on them.

I remember mostly going to the Strand Theatre on Sunday afternoon. You could see a movie and have popcorn and a coke all for twenty-five cents. They also had some beauty pageants at the theater.

I remember going to the Tot Shop looking at clothes and being helped by Gladys Frazier or Mrs. Anderson. I would go in Bowab's and look at dress patterns, and Hazel Davis would always be there willing to help. I really liked just going in all the stores and just looking around. I don't ever remember anyone minding me being there. I always felt welcome. I liked going across the street to the post office several times a day to get the mail. I liked just looking around at the posters. The mail was put up more than once a day.

[Bristow's Pharmacy was in a prime location, right in the middle of North Main Street, almost across from the post office. It was a good place for Beverly to see what was really going on in that block of downtown.]

LOWELL MCGILL

[Downtown Atmore in the 1940s, '50s, and '60s was certainly different from today as Lowell McGill wrote in a column for the Atmore Advance *on November 26, 2014. Part of that article is reprinted here.]*

Saturday strolls on South Main Street in the '40s and '50s. Of course the Strand was the main attraction with folks of all ages heading to this popular theater where movies were shown all day long and into the night. Along the way you would find Cliff Frazier standing outside Stallworth's Clothing Store, inviting customers in for some great bargains, and Gail Smith would throw open his Western Auto store where you could find everything from bicycles to refrigerators.

Lukie Anderson posted himself at the main door to his Anderson's Department Store, inviting customers to a full line of family clothing. On down the street at the Sweet Shop, delicious food cooking in the kitchen emitted an aroma that was just too difficult to pass by. Fred George at Atmore Hardware kept his store filled with not just hardware items, but toys and appliances as well.

On the same street prior to Agnes Smith's founding The Greater Fair, Nall's Family Grocery and the A&P flourished with weekly food bargains. Just across the street was Piggly Wiggly.

Customers often shopped Nall's to get a ten-cent pint of chocolate milk, which was displayed in an ice-filled cooler near the front door.

A trip to the movies also included a trip to Escambia

Drugs for a dime milkshake. Many high school boys and girls had part-time jobs here, but the store was generally noted for those pretty women who worked behind the counters. My sister-in-law, Margaret Lockwood, was one of them.

On the other side of South Main Street, Escambia Hardware offered a wonderful selection of hardware items and household furnishings as well. Mr. Lumpkin graciously fronted that store with his invitation to customers. Dr. Peavey maintained his medical practice on that same side of the street for several years.

One of the big problems on those busy Saturdays was finding a parking place. It would be difficult to imagine, unless you were there, the number of cars in town that day. Folks came from communities twenty-five to thirty miles away. There were so many cars that city policemen had to show them parking spaces on Atmore's side streets. Many folks came to town early just to find a cherished parking space.

Particularly in the 1940s and '50s, the Strand offered prizes from contests held on Saturday nights. One contest was called "Hot Seat." Patrons found seated in those designated seats when the numbers were called were awarded an assortment of prizes, such as free movie tickets, milkshakes and sandwiches from Escambia Drug Store, Reid Rexall Drug Store, and Bristow's Pharmacy. Other prizes were free dry cleaning from Bill O'Neal at John's Dry Cleaners, oil changes at Bricken Motors and R. Leon Jones Motor Company, a free bag of parched peanuts from Bristow's Pharmacy, a pair of baby shoes from the Cinderella Shoppe, a free haircut from Elite Barber Shop, and a free perm from Helen's Beauty Shop. A grand prize on occasions was a $25 shopping coupon at a local grocery store of your choice.

Kevin McKinley

One of my earliest memories of downtown was of a department store on South Main, where the thrift store is currently located. I can't remember the name, but they had a good toy section. As a small child, I always tried to manage a trip there when I could talk my mom into taking me.

My dad and I used a barber across the street from Peacock's barber shop on Ridgeley. His name escapes me now but there were two of them, his partner was an Odom. I always will remember going in the shop during the winter, and they had this huge gas heater, the kind with ceramic grates and a tin cup of water setting on the front of the heater (amazing what sticks out in memory of a kid).

We also shopped at Western Auto. One year my grandmother bought me a kid's fire truck that had the pedals, letters, whistle and all that. I was probably 5 but I'd bet there was no happier kid in Atmore, Canoe, or Robinsonville that day in 1975 or '76, (I was four or five).

In his book, *Shadows and Dust III: Legacies,* Kevin has this to say about Main Street in the "olden days":

North Main Street in Atmore was the hub of activity on Saturday afternoons. Model T Fords lined both sides of the street. An endless patchwork of black Ford automobiles lined every parking space with their black procession interrupted by farmers in bib overalls and straw hats crossing the streets along with businessmen in their gray and black woolen coats. All the while the money from cotton, corn, lumber and turpentine flowing in a stream of green into the coffers of the shop keepers who plied their trade in the crowded brick and mortar stores along the street.

Saturdays were special days in Atmore during this era in that most people in the surrounding area came into the town to do their shopping. Many would come early and stay all day.

Young girls, dressed in their finest outfits, would arrive with their parents and parade up and down the streets while their mothers shopped in the grocery stores and their fathers took care of "men's business" in the feed stores and barber shops.

During the 1920s, more than forty barber shops served the town. Under the barber's pole, the men of the area would sit in the tall chairs with their heads tucked back by a clean-cut barber while receiving a close shave by a steady hand. Meanwhile, the other patrons waited while indulging one another with quirky tales, the memory of which would soon evaporate in the room like snow on warm ground as the day wore on into evening.

Most stores on Main Street, particularly grocery stores, remained open until midnight. Farm workers and mill workers were always the last patrons to do their weekly shopping and therefore the stores made a special accommodation to their needs by extending their hours. Because of the extra hours, the downtown businesses usually closed on Thursdays at noon and kept longer hours on Saturday.

Families made a special event out of the Saturday shopping with many families bringing their lunch to town and picnicking on the back of their trucks or under a shade tree. Even though the hustle and bustle of the downtown went on well into the night, the Saturday business session did eventually come to a close. Sundays were quiet along the Main Street store fronts as the townspeople and country folks made their way to the sober, solid wooden church pews for worship the next morning.[33]

EDITH CRUIT MAYS

The Cruit family lived on present-day Pensacola Avenue, then called Mill Street because Carney Mill Company was at the end of the street. Edith Mays remembers the big pond and seeing logs coming down it.

At one time in Atmore's history, ice was delivered to area residents. The old delivery man would saw the ice into the size needed. Children would put their hands underneath and get the shavings to suck on. The milkman came daily, early in the morning, calling "Milk,

milk, cream and all." An empty bottle was swapped for a full one.

Entertainment was the picture show, without sound, and the drug store. Mrs. Mays went after school and would spend hours there before going home. Escambia Drug Store had a Victrola, and the students would dance. Coke floats were a favorite treat. A special service was the drive up. A toot of the horn would bring delivery service to your car.

Her mother did all of the shopping for the family, mainly at the Carney Mill Commissary and Bowab's. Edith Mays, meanwhile, was in school. The high school burned in 1925, the year she graduated, and the last part of her senior year was held at the First Baptist Church. Robert Hodnette would sit at the pulpit doing his work, and the smart students figured out a way to spy on him. They would send one student up to ask a question while Mr. Hodnette was making out a test. That student would look and see what page the book was open to so they could know what page to study for the test. Sometimes they slipped out the back door and went to town. When she graduated at sixteen, Mrs. Mays wore her first pair of hose and was pictured with her class on the front steps of the church.

Trains would come through town and stop for long periods of time. Mrs. Mays was often called a tomboy and wore overalls. This made it easy for her to crawl under the parked train to get to the other side.

Skating was a favorite pastime, and the sidewalk in front of the Baptist Church was where she learned to skate. She also enjoyed using "Tom Walkers" [stilts].

This native-born Atmorean also was proud to say that she never lived outside of Atmore except for the years she was away at college. This is remarkable because she lived to be 101 and her mother, Ada Cruit, lived to 103. Mays had a long time to look back and remember Atmore's history, from 1908 to 2009.

Curtis Parker

Some guys at school pulled a Halloween trick one year. They pulled a two-mule wagon all across town to the high school, where they disassembled it and put it behind the columns of the ECHS facade. Monday morning, Mr. Hodnette asked Mr. Barnes to have someone remove the wagon. Not so ironically, he picked the same three guys who put it there. They claimed that they knew nothing about taking a wagon apart but one of them was Leon Akins, a farm boy, and Mr. Barnes knew better. They had to disassemble and reassemble the wagon, since it would not fit between the columns—while the whole student body looked on, at recess, and then pull it all the way back thru town to the livery, in broad daylight.

Peacock's poolroom, which had only two tables, was behind Peacock's Barber Shop on Ridgeley Street, and could also be accessed by two doors at each end, opening to the alley. They probably sold beer too. I don't remember. It was not as teenage friendly as Stewart's Pool Room. There were also a few stores in the first NW block off Main, seems like a clothing store and a butcher shop. Houston Wolf operated one of them for a time—sold syrup in gallon cans and watermelons for as little as a quarter. As I remember, Tennant's Cafe was at the northwest corner of the first block, off Main. It was a large building— which may still exist. They probably sold a full menu of food.

The poolroom on Nashville was owned and operated by John Stewart and was managed by his bachelor brother-in-law John Mason Harvey. That poolroom spot is now empty. They did sell beer also but did not strictly enforce the Alabama seating rule for drinking beer. Strangers were told they had to be seated to be served, by law. I think you were supposed to be sixteen to enter the pool room, but that was not strictly enforced. The same is true for gambling. When the pros came into town, the gambling went on into the wee hours, with the police sometimes coming in to watch. I left there many nights at 2–3 a.m. The bets were often more than $200 a game. Typically, the pro would clean out a local farmer. Then John Harvey, called Little John by everyone because he was short, would take on the pro and usually cleaned him out. When the pool room burned, I sent a picture from the front page of the *Advance* to a friend with my caption, "Atmore pool hall burns. Hundreds of Atmore boys homeless."

Just for kicks, survey the main intersection of Main and Nashville Avenue. It is quite wide, but I remember there was a fire hydrant on the corner next to Elmore's that was taken out by Hugh Dickson's trucks from Monroeville trying to make the turn towards Mobile with logs so long that they sometimes took out the railroad warning that stood on the southeast side of the tracks. I understood the "virgin pine" logs were used for pilings in New Orleans.

Somewhere, I have a picture of a power pole (all poles in Lower Alabama are commonly called "telephone" poles) in the center of that intersection that was used like an English "round-a-bout." My brother-in-law, Troy Hopkins, remembered it still being there when he drove a gasoline tanker for Graham Oil Company at the age of fifteen. It must have been around 1942–43.

There was a livery stable on Ridgeley Street, and the people who came into town by mule and wagon used to keep the mules tied up in that general area. The country folks seemed to hang out mainly in the north part of town, as I remember, but I don't know.

There was an alley behind the C. K. Carter store that accessed a barber shop and a pool room. One, or both, was owned by a Peacock. That alley went all the way through to the street beside the railroad track where another barber shop, I think Elite, was located, along with Graham-Brooks Wholesale. I remember Tennant's Cafe run by Treetop (Alton) Tennant, where they sold catfish and beer. There, and the pool room, were the only places in town that I remember selling beer.

Past the livery was a blacksmith shop run by June Kizer. He was a friend of my dad and let me hang out there and turn the crank on his coal fired forge. Across the street, on the corner, was Carden Milling Company. People brought their corn in to have it ground into cornmeal.

There was also Atmore Recap Shop, owned by Bill Varner. Jack Stallworth had a tractor dealership there also, which later became Hendrix Tractor. Then there was nothing but cotton warehouses until a cotton gin was built across the street. That newer gin was the first to handle "pulled" cotton versus picked, and then machine picked. It could better separate the husks and burrs, but the picked cotton still brought a better price. The Atmore Truckers Association was there with its milling operation, peanut warehouse, potato shed, etc.

Further down was the "Sale Pen" where they auctioned off cattle. After the Frisco Railroad trestle was Wilson Avenue, and it was residential.

MARCIA WEBB PEPPERMAN

My grandmother, Mrs. Alfred Pellar Webb, lived at 205 N. Main Street, and, on the day I was born, she drove my mother to the Atmore General Hospital where Dr. J. O. Lisenby brought me into this world. My mother always said she worried that we might not make it to the hospital because grandmother Ida learned to drive as a much older woman and wasn't that good at it.

Main Street was my world. My grandmother's house was the first residence on the left going north and it had been there since the original owner, Dr. J. F. Peavy, built it around the turn of the twentieth century. The sidewalks in front were part of the yard, and they ran both north and south. I don't remember how old I was before I was able to walk without an adult all the way through town and across the L&N Railroad tracks to South Main where my uncle Pellar Webb had a hardware store. Across the street from his store sat my great-grandmother Abbie Stewart's house. It was a two-story wooden house that had been there fifty plus years but eventually was torn down, and a bank was built in its place.

I don't remember too much about my great-grandmother's house. She was no longer living when I was born. Her youngest daughter, Ava, lived in the house as a single woman. Her mother called her Babe so we called her Aunt Babe. She was a school teacher and loved children. She had pet names for all her nieces and nephews. My dad, whose name was Tom, was Tommy Tucker (a nursery rhyme).

I only lived in Atmore for a couple of short periods of time, but our family visited a lot. And so my memories spill out over many wonderful years. The extended family was a large one, and I had many cousins. Some of them lived in Atmore but mostly in other states, and it was at my grandmother's house that we would see each other.

The upstairs of her house had two large bedrooms and two small ones. My sisters and I always shared one of the large bedrooms. There was one on the front that faced Main Street. Back then, we slept with the windows open so we hopefully might catch a little breeze. The yard had several large oak trees which shaded the house with the branches spreading out in all directions. We spent many a summer night hoping for a little breeze and praying that we didn't have a mosquito in the room.

There were two very familiar sounds that I remember so well there on Main Street. One was the trains that came through town at all hours of the night and day. The other sound was the big trucks that passed right by the house night and day. They were relentless. They were much louder than the trains because they were so close to the house, but we finally got used to them.

Going to the picture show was one of my favorite things to do, and The Strand was only a couple of blocks south on Main. *Gone with the Wind* was one of the most memorable movies that played there, and I saw it many times. One of the nice memories of The Strand was how clean it was and never very crowded. To me, it was like a big-city theater nestled in a small town.

The longest period of time that I actually lived in Atmore was the fall of 1961, when I was a freshman at the junior high school. We had moved from Oklahoma to Alabama and were living with my grandmother when school started. I didn't know anyone my age, but as luck would have it, another family had just moved to Atmore and they had a daughter my age. Our Atmore relatives knew each other, and that is how I met my first friend, Nancy (Bosenberg) Karrick. She was also living with her grandmother whose house was on Pensacola Avenue, and it was within walking distance down Main Street as well as practically across from the junior high school. I always walked to school mornings and afternoons, rain or shine.

The Atmore Hardware was a hangout for my family in later years after we moved to Bay Minette. Saturday was our day to visit the folks in Atmore, and we would usually walk there from my grandmother's house. The Atmore Hardware was very unique in that it had old wooden floors that creaked with every step, a potbellied stove in the back for heat and a huge nail bin that spun around. On the shelves up at the front of the store were colorful Fiesta dishes for sale. On Saturday mornings, my Aunt Letha and her sister, Pearl Williams, along with their mother, Mrs. Lackey, would park in front of the store and visit with all the folks that would be walking by. It was a tradition.

Back then, before there were shopping malls, people went to town. Main Street was the place to be and it was full of energy and excitement. I'm glad it was a part of my life.

Anna Bell Quarker

Anna Bell Quarker was ninety-seven years old when I talked to her in 2007. She had come to Atmore from Uriah when she was thirteen. She recounted that the stores in town were all busy, and you could buy whatever you wanted in town. She frequented Grimsley's, Bowab's, and C. K. Carter. Going to town meant a ride in a wagon on Friday or Saturday. Corn was taken to the grist mill to be ground into meal.

The family grew their own vegetables and raised meat. They had milk, butter, and made lard from hogs. They didn't grow wheat for flour or sugar and had to buy those items. Flour came in sacks with pretty designs and she would get fifty-pound sacks in order to have enough material to make a dress. She made her own patterns when the children were little and later bought some.

Having eleven children meant lots of clothes to wash. Water was gotten from a pump, heated to boiling, and a stick was used to push them down. Clothes were rinsed in cold water then hung on the line to try.

Cooking was done on a wood stove. "I wish I had me a wood stove now. It's slow and takes time cooking and food tastes better," was her comment. That method was the forerunner of the crock pot.

Baths were taken in a #3 tub with the water changed after each child had bathed. With eleven children, bath time was a lengthy process.

Ruthie Mae Rackard

Ruthie Mae Rackard was one of thirteen children, and Calvin McGhee was her brother. Going to town meant piling into a wagon pulled by a mule. The wagon was parked near Atmore Truckers. The family mostly went to town on Saturday, but sometimes would go during the week. Her parents traded at C. K. Carter's and would buy dry goods and groceries. She remembered buying fabric on bolts for clothing.

Bowab's, located right down the street, was often another stop for the family. She remembered some of the streets being paved with bricks.

School for the McGhee children was at Bell Creek Church, about four miles from home. There was no lunchroom, and the children had to carry their lunches. She attended school only through the sixth grade because Indian children were not allowed to go to school in Atmore or McCullough. School meant walking four to five miles as well as going to a neighbor's house across the road to get water for the students to drink.

Howard Shell

Howard Shell, who served as mayor of Atmore for many years, had some tidbits of information about the city facilities. He started by saying that Mr. S. L. Rollins was the city clerk, and Miss Bertha Lynch was the utilities clerk way back when. In the old city hall, on the right side, were teller-like windows where bills were paid. Abner and Bea Jernigan lived in back of city hall. He was the fire chief. John Garrard was on the building committee for the new city hall complex.

Gainus' Blacksmith Shop was behind C. K. Carter's store in the late 1930s or early '40s. The area behind the Legion Building was a cypress pond. He recalled people coming into town in a wagon which was pulled by mules. They were tied up at one of the vacant lots or livery stables. The Greater Fair corner was home to Lamont and Sowell Garage and Mr. Cobb, his father-in-law, worked there in the late 1930s to early '40s.

Bateson's opened in 1946, and moved to its new location in 1966. They closed in 2006. The Crook Hotel was built in the early 1900s by William Carney and known as the Carney Hotel. George Crook bought it about 1924.

Later, it was known as the Norman and then Burton Hotel. It was torn down in 1960 to make way for the new Bank of Atmore.

Shell remembered Escambia Hardware begun in the early 1920s by Robert Cruit and H. W. Currie. In 1918 W. R. Maxwell and E. F. Goldsmith purchased an insurance company which morphed into Maxwell-Haley and then Maxwell, Haley, & Castleberry Insurance.

Clint Turner

Clint Turner, who was born in 1915, said that the town was called Williams' Station when his daddy first came. In fact, one day his daddy went to Williams' Station to get supplies, and the name had been changed to Atmore. He would take young Clint into town in a mule and buggy. "Atmore was a big pond back in those days," said Mr. Turner.

Carney had two ponds for logs and a sawmill. His father would put a bale of cotton on the wagon, and Clint sat on top and chewed a stalk of cane the three to four hours it took to get from Robinsonville to Atmore. Main Street consisted of mud holes. There were no sidewalks, and bricks were put about three feet in front of the stores for a road. The bricks were made out from Flomaton. Horses, buggies, mules, wagons, and oxen would go down the street. There were also lots of big houses along South Main Street.

Charlie Ware

[Charlie Ware wrote his memories of downtown Atmore for an article in the October 2015 atmore Magazine. *Reprinted here, with his permission, is most of that article.]*

I walked out of the post office on a Saturday morning a few weeks ago and paused on the steps for a few minutes to look around at the half dozen or so cars parked along the entire length of Main Street and at the one other person on the sidewalk. I couldn't help recalling what Saturday was like in downtown Atmore when I was a kid back in the 1950s. This was long before giant shopping centers, Walmart, Internet shopping, and before most families had a television.

Everybody for miles around came to town on Saturday, whether to shop, socialize, or just to watch the other people and be part of the action. The sidewalks and stores were always crowded, and there was a festive air up and down the street. You could always count on meeting your friends somewhere in town on Saturday.

People who drove to town tried to come early to get a good parking spot. Parking at that time was diagonal to the curb so that more cars could be parked along each street, but by midmorning, people were driving around and around looking for a place to park. When someone got a spot, they were probably going to be there for the entire day. Those who came late would have to park on a back street or at the Byrne Field parking lot.

During this time, there were still a number of people who came to town by mule and wagon. There was a location near the old Merriwether feed barn at Trammell and Ridgeley streets where wagons were parked and mules could be fed and watered.

Both Main Street and Nashville Avenue were lined with stores. I would estimate that within a block from the center of town there were at least sixty retail businesses, and you could get anything you needed right in downtown Atmore. Those stores did most of their business on Saturday and would be open from 8 a.m. until at lest 7 p.m. to accommodate the crowds.

There were six grocery stores right in the heart of town on the main streets and several others along the side streets. Today, looking at the buildings that housed those stores, it is hard to believe that you could actually find almost every grocery item you may need. None of those stores were as large as the frozen food section at a modern supermarket, but they were fully stocked and even had butcher counters where you could have meat cut to order. They also had bag-boys who would bag your groceries and take them out to the car for you.

Those who didn't need to shop would just stroll the sidewalks, window shop, and chat with friends they would meet. Some would just sit in their cars and watch all the activity on the streets. There were always several cars where groups of men would sit on the fenders and tell stories. During football season, big crowds would gather around the few cars that had radios.

The sidewalks of North Main were always littered with peanut shells. Those peanuts came from Bristow's Pharmacy, where a peanut roaster operated all day long. Roasted peanuts were a fixture downtown, and it seemed everywhere you looked folks were munching hot peanuts from the little brown bags from Bristow's.

If you preferred popcorn, you could get it from the Strand Theatre through the ticket window without having to go into the lobby. J&K dime store also had a popcorn machine on the sidewalk.

There was no shortage of refreshment since, in addition to Bristow's, Reid Rexall and Escambia pharmacies all had wonderful soda fountains where you could get a Coke or a cone of ice cream for a nickel. For twenty cents, you could get an ice cream soda or, for a quarter, a giant milkshake. A milkshake contained at least six scoops of ice cream and was made in a big tin cup which was enough to fill two tall glasses. Buster's ice cream parlor on the second block of South Main had an even larger variety of treats and snacks. The best hamburgers were at the Tiny Diner on West Nashville Avenue or at the bus station cafe.

There were also two bakeries on South Main just across the street from each other, where hot doughnuts and other delicious goodies were available. (When I questioned Charlie about the two bakeries, he confirmed one was the Atmore Bakery on the east side of the street and the other was Knoblock's on the west, which was in a little building that adjoined the Sweet Shop and which later became part of the Sweet Shop.)

On Saturday, the Strand Theatre opened in the

morning and stayed open until around midnight. It was usually packed. There would be a double feature movie, several cartoons, and a serial short playing nonstop all day long. Admission was ten cents for kids and twenty-five cents for adults. Parents could drop off their kids for a day of entertainment and give them a quarter which would be enough for admission plus a drink and popcorn.

For some of the men and older boys, entertainment meant the pool hall. Atmore had three pool halls right in the middle of town, and there was often a long wait for a table on Saturday afternoon. The pool hall was a dark and cool place to hang out on a hot day. I would often slip into the pool hall but only after carefully scanning up and down the street to make sure nobody I knew would see me go in.

For several years, there was a shooting gallery that would come into town on Saturday. It was mounted on a trailer and would park next to Claude Peacock's Barber Shop on Ridgeley Street. You could stand there on the sidewalk and fire a .22 rifle at playing cards, trying to shoot the spots out of the card. There were prizes to be won such as watches, radios, and stuffed animals, but I never saw anyone win anything. They apparently didn't take very good care of their rifles because the sights always seemed to be a little bent.

The beauty and barber shops always did well on Saturday and would sometimes be open until late at night to take care of all the customers. I remember there were four barber shops in the center of town, and they were a favorite hangout for men to gather to tell jokes or fishing and hunting stories. It would usually be standing room only.

All of the barber shops had shoeshine stands where men could get their shoes shined up for Sunday church. There was also a stand on the sidewalk in front of Reid Rexall store that was open on Sunday morning for that last-minute shine.

Another feature that added to the festive atmosphere of those Saturdays was street musicians. There were often groups on the sidewalks playing musical instruments and singing. I remember one group of four or five people who played accordions. For years, there was a blind man who sang and played the guitar as he strolled along north Main Street.

No Saturday downtown would be complete without the street preachers. Preachers would stake out busy street corners and would preach for hours at a time, sometimes to a small crowd that would gather but often just to people who were passing by. I recall a preacher one day at the corner of Main Street and Nashville Avenue who preached nonstop for over four hours.

As the day wound down and the street lights began coming on and all the shopping and socializing was done, families would start to gather back at their cars, and most would head for home. For some, there would be dinner at the Sweet Shop, the City Cafe, or one of the other cafes that remained open late on Saturday night.

There was usually a dance or an all-night singing at the American Legion hall.

During the summer months, Atmore's semipro baseball team would probably be playing at Byrne Field. Some teenagers, those lucky ones whose parents would let them, would go to the John Dixon record hop at the National Guard Armory. My parents wouldn't let me go.

Another source of Saturday night entertainment that was unique to the 1950s was available at Watson Hardware store on North Main. When Watson's closed for the night, a television, with a speaker wired to the outside, was left playing in the front window. Most people didn't have television in their home, but they were welcome to come sit on the sidewalk and watch television through the store window. People came prepared with blankets to spread on the sidewalks or with lawn chairs. Some even brought dinner. They would spend the evening watching such programs as "Gunsmoke," "Have Gun, Will Travel," and "Saturday Night Wrestling" through the widescreen twenty-one-inch black-and-white television.

This is just a jumble of a few of the memories I have of those Saturdays of so long ago. The best memories are not of specific people or events, but of the feeling, the excitement, the festival-like atmosphere that came over the city on those days of hustle and bustle when everybody came to town. I'm sure that all who were around at that time have their own special memories of those wonderful days when downtown Atmore was so alive.[34]

Bibliography and Notes

UNPUBLISHED MATERIALS

Anderson, Lucine "Lukie" and Mirtis. Multiple interviews by author, 1990–2013, Atmore, Alabama.

Bailey, Ellie. Interviewed by author, May 15, 2017, Atmore, Alabama.

Barron, Raymond. Interviewed by author, March, 2007, Atmore, Alabama.

Birnberg, Helaine Danziger. Interviewed by author, June 4, 2007, Atmore, Alabama.

Bosenberg, Charles Ellsworth. Multiple interviews by author, 1995–2000, Atmore, Alabama.

Bosenberg, Velma Carter. Multiple interviews by author, 1995–2006, Atmore, Alabama.

Brooks, R. W. "Early History of Atmore," as told to Robert Hodnette Jr., 1927.

Chapman, Bill and Nancy. Interviewed by author, July 21, 2006, Atmore, Alabama.

Crook, Elise. Interviewed by author, July 3, 2005, Atmore, Alabama.

Crook, Mattie Lou. Interviewed by author, July 13, 2006, Atmore, Alabama.

Day, Joel and Louise. Interviewed by author, December 26, 2009, Atmore, Alabama.

Dunaway, Mildred Carter. Multiple interviews by author, 1990–1998, Atmore, Alabama.

Earle, Margarette. Interviewed by author, July 12, 2006, Atmore, Alabama.

Ellison, Linda Lumpkin. Interviewed by author, March 21, 2021, Atmore, Alabama.

Fischer, Lawrence Eugene. Interviewed by author, December 30, 1998, Atmore, Alabama.

Forte, James. Interviewed by author, July 20, 2006, Atmore, Alabama.

Frazier, Cliff and Gladys. Interviewed by author, July 22, 2006, Atmore, Alabama.

Godwin, Willena. Interviewed by author, July 25, 2006, Atmore, Alabama.

Hammack, Drunetta. Interviewed by author, August 16, 2009, Atmore, Alabama.

Jernigan, Glenn and Mary. Interviewed by author, March, 2007, Atmore, Alabama.

Jenko, Carolyn Fischer. Multiple email and phone interviews by author, 1995–2020.

Karrick, Nancy, Gloria Marshall Jones, and Sherry Digmon, *Reflections: Conversations With Some Of Atmore's Senior Citizens.* Atmore, Alabama: Barnett & Associates, 2007.

Kennington, Albert. Interviewed by author, July 25, 2020, Atmore, Alabama.

King, Pamela, consultant. "Atmore Historical Survey: Building Descriptions of Properties Within the Proposed Atmore Historical District," Birmingham, Alabama: P. S. King Associates, 2000.

Latino, Bonnie Bartel. Interviewed by author July 29, 2020, Atmore, Alabama.

Liles, Owen and Virginia. Interviewed by author, August 2, 2007, Bay Minette, Alabama.

Lufkin, Jack Curtis. Multiple interviews by author, April 26, 2009-February 2021, Atmore, Alabama.

Lucas, Ethel. Interviewed by author, March, 2007, Atmore, Alabama.

Lumpkin, Helen Ramsey. Interviewed by author, July 19, 2006, Atmore, Alabama.

Lumpkin, Jim. Interviewed by author on March 22, 2021, by phone from Selma, Alabama.

Lundberg, Beverly Bristow. Interviewed by author, September 19, 2020, Atmore, Alabama.

McCoy, Thera Kelly. Interviewed by author, June 28, 2001, Atmore, Alabama.

McGill, Lowell and Ouida. Interviewed by author, February 13, 2015, Atmore, Alabama.

McKinley, Kevin. Interviewed by author July 29, 2020, Atmore, Alabama.

Maxwell, Robert and Hattie. Interviewed by author, July 19, 2006, Atmore, Alabama.

Mays, Edith Cruit. Interviewed by author, March, 2007, Atmore, Alabama.

Middleton, Haskew and Gladys. Interviewed by author, July 22, 2006, Atmore, Alabama.

Norris, Edgar and Molly. Interviewed by author, August 1, 2011, Atmore, Alabama.

Parker, Curtis. Interviewed by author, October 16, 2020, Atmore, Alabama.

Pepperman, Marcia Webb. Interviewed by author, September 20, 2011, Bay Minette, Alabama.

Quarker, Annie Bell. Interviewed by author, March, 2007, Atmore, Alabama.

Rackard, Ruthie Mae. Interviewed by author, March, 2007, Atmore, Alabama.

Sharpless, Virginia. Interviewed by author, July 30, 2020, Atmore, Alabama.

Shell, Howard. Interviewed by author, July 25, 2006, Atmore, Alabama.

Shiver, John and Myrtle. Interviewed by author, March 25, 2007, Atmore, Alabama.

Staff, Ann Hoehn. Interviewed by author, July 21, 2006, Atmore, Alabama.

Swift, Byard. Interviewed by author, July 28, 2008, Atmore, Alabama.

Swift, Lucille King. Interviewed by author, November 13, 2007, Atmore, Alabama.

Thomas, Nell. Interviewed by author, July 20, 2006, Atmore, Alabama.

Threadgill, Patricia Crook. Interviewed by author July 13, 2006, Atmore, Alabama.

Turner, Clint. Interviewed by author, March, 2007, Atmore, Alabama.

Vickery, Dana. Interviewed by author, March 21, 2019, Atmore, Alabama.

Ware, Charlie. Interviewed by author July 28, 2020, Atmore, Alabama.

Webb, John. Interviewed by author, February 11, 2006, Atmore, Alabama.

Whitten, Annie Ruth. Interviewed by author, July 3, 2005, Atmore, Alabama.

Theses and Dissertations

Bates, Maisie F. "History of Atmore, Alabama." Course assignment, Livingston Normal, Livingston, Alabama, 1925.

Yancey, William Hugo. "The History of Atmore, Alabama, and Surrounding Area." Master's thesis, Alabama Polytechnic Institute, Auburn, Alabama, 1943.

Newspapers and Periodicals

The Atmore Advance. 1927–2021.

Atmore News, 2005–2021.

The Atmore Record. 1912–1922.

The Atmore Spectrum. 1903–1912.

Photographs

Ditto Gorme

Nancy Karrick

Secondary Sources

Atmore Area Chamber of Commerce. *A Pictorial Look at Atmore's Early History.* Atmore, Alabama: Atmore Area Chamber of Commerce, nd.

Atmore Telephone Directory. Atmore, Alabama: Atmore Telephone Company, 1941.

Bailey, Anne Sledge. *Buildings of Greensboro.* Self published, 2011.

Corman, W. F. *Magneto, Common Battery & Dial.* Self published, nd.

Karrick, Charles Ernest. *History of the Bank of Atmore.* Montgomery, Alabama: NewSouth Books, 2004.

Lester, Marjorie. *Memories of Banbury*. Self published, 1986.

McKinley, Kevin. *Shadows and Dust III: Legacies*. Morris, North Carolina: Lulu Publications, 2018.

Parker, Curtis A. *Where the Rails Crossed*. Self published, nd.

Pepperman, Marcia Webb. *Grace Was In Their Steps*. Self published, 2011.

Polk's Atmore City Directory 1963–64. Richmond, Virginia: R. L. Polk & Company, 1964.

Polk's Atmore City Directory 1988. Richmond, Virginia: R. L. Polk & Company, 1988.

Polk's Atmore City Directory 1989. Richmond, Virginia: R. L. Polk & Company, 1989.

Waters, Annie C. *History of Escambia County Alabama*. Spartanburg, South Carolina: The Reprint Company, 1993.

Endnotes

1. Nancy Bosenberg Karrick, "For God and Country," *atmore Magazine*, February 2006, 18–21.
2. Ibid.
3. Nancy Bosenberg Karrick, "From Birth Until …" *atmore Magazine*, November 2011, 10–12.
4. Nancy Bosenberg Karrick, "Sweet Shop Building," *atmore Magazine*, September 2009, 16–19.
5. *Atmore Advance*, "75th Anniversary Celebrated by Atmore Hardware," February 1, 1973.
6. *Atmore Advance*, "Some of Atmore's First Stores," August 25, 1949, 1.
7. Nancy Bosenberg Karrick, "The Picture Show," *atmore Magazine*, October 2008, 16–19.
8. *Lowell McGill*, "Strand Was a Place of Lots of My Memories," *Atmore Advance*, November 20, 2013.
9. *Atmore Advance*, "Making Its Mark," April 6, 2019, 6.
10. Nancy Bosenberg Karrick, "Watch Where You're Going," *atmore Magazine*, August 2019, 25.
11. Nancy Bosenberg Karrick, "Escambia Drug Store," *atmore Magazine*, June 2007, 24–27.
12. Nancy Bosenberg Karrick, "Watch Where You're Going," *atmore Magazine*. August 2019, 24–25.
13. Ibid., 21–22.
14. Charles Karrick, *History of the Bank of Atmore*. Montgomery: NewSouth Books, 2004, 27.
15. Ibid., 4.
16. *Atmore Record*, January 6, 1921, 5
17. *Atmore Advance Progress 2019*, "Earle's Jewelers Was a Mainstay Here," April 6, 2019, 36.
18. Nancy Bosenberg Karrick, "Dixie Blend—'It's Always Fresh,'" *atmore Magazine*, May 2019, 20–23.
19. Marcia Webb Pepperman, *Grace Was In Their Steps*. Self, 2011, 31–35.
20. William Hugo Yancey, "The History of Atmore, Alabama, and Surrounding Area," masters thesis, Auburn, Alabama: Alabama Polytechnic Institute, 1943, 44.
21. *Washington Post*. "On President's Day, Why Not Make a George Washington Pie?," February 19, 2017.
22. Sherry Digmon. "The Letter Box," *atmore Magazine*, June 2002, 15.
23. Sherry Digmon. "The Liles Building," *atmore Magazine*, August 2017, 16.
24. Karrick. *History of the Bank of Atmore*. 4.
25. Ibid., 27.
26. Ibid., 76–77.
27. Ibid., 97–98.
28. Ibid., 122.
29. *Atmore Advance*, "Bank Traces History to 1915," July 2, 1970, 2B.
30. Lance Blackburn, "First National Bank & Trust Through the Years," *atmore Magazine*, August 2007, 17.
31. W. F. Corman. "*Magneto, Common Battery & Dial.*" nd, 15–16.
32. Yancey, 46.
33. Kevin McKinley, *Shadows and Dust III: Legacies*. Morris, North Carolina: Publications, 2018, 123.
34. Ware, Charlie, *atmore Magazine*, October, 2015, 12–14.

About the Author

NANCY KARRICK was born in Atmore, Alabama, and though she spent the first few years of her life in Pensacola, Florida, she spent most weekends and summers in Atmore before her family moved back home. After graduating from high school in Atmore, she attended Auburn University and earned a degree in elementary education, then received a master's in library science from Florida State University.

During her late husband Charles's twenty-one-year career in the military, she had the opportunity to live in Georgia, Arizona, Oklahoma, New York, Hawaii, Korea, Morocco, and Belgium, and to travel in many other countries. In fact, she has been in all fifty of the United States, as well as in sixty-seven countries on all seven continents.

She has worked as a medical librarian at the United States Military Academy, as a school librarian at all age levels in the United States and Belgium, and taught fourth grade, retiring from teaching in 2012. She is a member of Beta Phi Mu, Kappa Delta Pi, Delta Kappa Gamma, Alpha Delta Kappa, and Kappa Kappa Iota, and served as Alabama state president of Delta Kappa Gamma.

Nancy is a fifty-eight-year member of Girl Scouts, thirty-plus year volunteer with American Red Cross, writer for *atmore Magazine,* member of American Legion and Veterans of Foreign Wars Ladies Auxiliaries, Atmore Lions Club, the First Baptist Church, Daughters of the American Revolution, and several other genealogical organizations.

Honors received include Girl Scout Thanks Badge, Red Cross Clara Barton Medal, Daughters of the American Revolution Community Service Award, Molly Pitcher Award for service to the Fort Sill, Oklahoma, community, and the Atmore Lion of the Year.

Nancy enjoys cross-stitch and embroidery, travel, reading, and cooking. She spends her spare time reading about historical subjects and trying new recipes.

She has one daughter and three grandchildren.

Facing page: Mid-twentieth century aerial view of downtown Atmore, with an arrow pointing to the author's family store, C.K.Carter General Merchandise.

Index

A

Abbie's Millinery Shop 51
ABC Store 19, 86, 92, 93
Ace Hardware 84
A Cut Above 77
Adams, Betty 111
Adams, Floyd 73, 74
Adams, Herman 73
Adams, J. B. "Burl" 69, 73, 74, 77
Adams, Josephine 73, 74
Adams Plaza 73
Agnes's Beauty Shop 48
Akins, Leon 136
Alabama Aluminum and Vinyl Products 63
Alabama Archery Academy 81
Alabama Citizens for Life of Escambia County 94
Alabama Department of Archives and History ix
Alabama Dry Goods 57
Alabama National Guard 93
Alabama Power Company 83
Alabama Roasters 77
Alabama Supreme Court 87
Alabama Wing House 63
Ala-Flora Fair 120, 122
Albert, Catherine 58
Albert, Jo 70
Albert's Cafe 57, 109
Albert's grocery 70
Albert's Restaurant 44
Albert, Toad 52
Albert, Tony 50, 52, 118
Alcoholic Beverage Control Board 93
Alfa Insurance 129
Alston, Theodore Shields 67, 75
Alston Wholesale Candy Distributors 67, 75
American Legion Building 18–20, 125, 140
American Red Cross 91, 113
American Tae Kwan Do 63
Amtrak 45, 95, 96
Anchor Cafe 77
Anderson Building 31
Anderson, Carl 23, 41, 101, 102
Anderson, Daulton 30, 33
Anderson, David 33
Anderson, James 32
Anderson, Lukie 19, 21, 22, 30, 31, 32, 33, 84, 88, 91, 113, 133
Anderson, Mary B. (Snookie) 23, 52, 53, 101
Anderson, Mirtis 19, 22, 25, 30, 31, 32, 56, 113, 133
Anderson's Department Store 32, 124, 133
Anderson's Photo Shop 101
Annie's Community Cup 63
Ann Marie Nowak Confidential Counseling Services 91
Ann's Barber Shop 92
Antiques and Collectibles 78
Antiques and Other Fine Things 57
A&P grocery 24, 41, 133
Ashley Street 46, 81
Atmorala 75, 82, 84, 88
Atmore Advance 29, 30, 32, 57, 65, 92, 109, 111, 113, 133, 137
Atmore, Alabama
  centennial of 115
  founding of 3, 45
  location of 4
  population of 3, 4
Atmore All Star Cheer and Dance 75
Atmore Appliances 110
Atmore Bakery 111, 142
Atmore ball park 122
Atmore Beauty Supply 91
Atmore Cafe 101
Atmore Carpet 61, 86, 103
Atmore Chamber of Commerce 4, 65, 66, 79, 93
Atmore, Charles Pawson 3
Atmore City Hall 18, 94, 97, 106, 120, 128
Atmore city park 119
Atmore Civil Defense 94
Atmore Coffee Company 64, 69, 73–74, 77
Atmore, C. P. 45
Atmore Dry Cleaners 99
Atmore Equipment 70
Atmore Farm & Garden 43
Atmore Finance Company 60
Atmore fire department 119, 126, 140
Atmore Flower Shop 22
Atmore Food Store 62
Atmore General Hospital 138
The Atmore (hotel) 3
Atmore Hardware 3, 17, 19, 20, 27–28, 108, 124, 127, 133, 139
atmore Magazine 22, 57, 90, 106, 141, 147
Atmore News 22
Atmore Office and School Supply 54, 125
Atmore pool 119
Atmore Post Office 60, 79, 84, 85, 87, 125, 132
Atmore Public Library 18, 20, 60, 94, 125
Atmore Realty 54, 65
Atmore Recap Shop 138
Atmore Record x, 127
Atmore Record Building 18
Atmore Rug and Shade 20
Atmore Spectrum x, 3, 61
Atmore Telephone Company 113
Atmore Truckers 140
Atmore Truckers Association 138
Atmore Video 61
Atmore Warehouse Company 65
Atmore Welcome Center 4
Aunt Hattie's Restaurant 103
Ayres Forestry 91

B

Bailey Communications Services 48
Bailey, Ellie 22, 38, 41, 53, 79, 85, 87, 92, 98, 99, 100
Ballard, J. F. 32
Ballard, J. T. 33, 36
Ballard, Mr. 83
Bank of Atmore ix, 18, 53, 60, 61, 65, 78, 104, 125, 129, 141
Baptists 19, 57, 79, 126, 127, 128, 136
barbers 39, 47, 51, 70, 71, 78, 92, 97, 109, 110, 130, 134, 135, 137, 143
Bargain TV Sales and Service 40
Barker's Grocery 101
Barnes, Mr. 136
Barnett and Associates 55
Barnett building 107
Barnett, Farrar 44
Barnett, Gilbert 106
Barnett, Henry 21
Barnett, Ken 33, 35
Barnett, Ned 113
Barnett's Standard 113
Barnett, Wayne 33
Barron, Raymond 115–144

Bartel, Bill 128
baseball 81, 144
Bateson's Furniture 41, 82, 140
Bateson's Too 39
Bay Minette, Alabama 19, 46, 74, 139
Beans Store 22
beauty shops 24, 38, 39, 77, 108, 110, 130, 143
Beauty Supply 64
Beck, Jack 98, 99, 100, 101, 102, 109
Bedsole's 62, 125
Bell Creek Church 140
Bell, Jessie 112
Bell, Jim 41, 78, 82
Beltone Hearing Aids 101
Ben Franklin store 60–61, 125, 132
Benison, Bubber 127
Benneson's 62, 127
Benton, Chester 19
Bethea, Cliff 24, 100, 101
Bethea, Pee Wee 24
Bethea's Grocery 100, 101, 125
Betty's 33
Betty's Dress Shop 59
Betty's Women's Clothes 38
Bill's Billiard Parlor 102
Bill's Dollar Store 78
Birnberg, Helaine Danziger 19, 57, 58, 67, 96, 115–116
Blossom Gas Company 92
Blue Devils. *See* Escambia County High School
bomb shelter 87
Bon Marche Dress Shop 54, 127
Booker Barber Shop 20
Boone's Cafe 102
Booneville, Alabama 74
Bosenberg, Charles 21, 37, 64, 66, 87, 96, 109

Bosenberg, Nancy. *See* Karrick, Nancy B.
Bosenberg, Velma Carter 19, 21, 23, 24, 37, 39, 64, 66, 85, 96, 102, 108, 109, 116–118, 119
Bowab, Blanche 104
Bowab, Bubba 59
Bowab, George 32, 104
Bowab's 62, 115, 125, 133, 136, 139, 140
Bowab, Selma 59
Boys Lard Collection 19
Bradford, Massey 61, 63, 64
Bradford's Grocery Store 63, 64
Brantley, Robert Earle 52
Brantley, Sallie M. 112
Brantley Tires 41
Brantley, Walter Scott 112
Bray, Mary 88
Breckenridge, Terrence 41
Brewton, Alabama 32, 35, 43, 46, 54, 65, 73, 74
Bricken Motors 134
Brislin, Harry 101
Brislin's Cleaners 101
Bristow, Claude 55
Bristow's Pharmacy 52, 55, 124, 125, 128, 133, 134, 142
Brooks, Leon 43, 44, 91
Brown, Agnes 51
Brown, Alfred 99
Brown, Bill 99, 101, 103
Brown Construction Company 101
Brown, R. L. 70, 78
Bryars, Clarence 35, 36
Bumann, Linda 58
Burger King 42
Burton Hotel 104, 119, 141
Bus Station 103
Buster's ice cream parlor 142

Byrne Field 73, 118, 120, 141, 144
Byrne, Sam 103

C

Calvert, Alabama 79
Canoe, Alabama 73, 134
Carden Milling Company 137
Carl's Decorating Services 61
Carney, Alice 79
Carney Hotel 140
Carney Lodge 18
Carney Logging 87
Carney Mill ii, 38, 53, 81, 87, 92, 94, 109, 125, 126, 129, 135, 141
Carney Mill Commissary 37, 115, 126, 127, 129, 130, 136
Carney Store 3, 38
Carney Street 128
Carney, William M. 24, 29, 45, 80, 140
Carol's Curiosity Shop 78
Carps Department Store 63
Carrier Air Conditioning 91
Carter Building 65
Carter, Charlie 65
Carter, Comer Knight 42, 44, 64, 65–68, 69, 75, 85, 117, 119, 120, 124
Carter, Daisy 65
Carter, Ed 64, 65, 68, 117
Carter, Mary. *See* Rabon, Mary Carter
Carter, Mildred. *See* Dunaway, Mildred Carter
Carter, Nancy Brantley 38, 65–68, 69, 93, 102, 108, 109, 119, 120
Carter, Ryan 22
Carter's Corner 66
Carter's Store. *See* C. K. Carter General Merchandise
Carter, Velma. *See* Bosenberg, Velma Carter

Carter, Zelma 64, 65, 67, 117
Castleberry, Keith 44, 53
Central Farm Supply 43
Chapman, Bill 22, 38, 81, 84, 86, 112
Chapman, Dr. 89, 90, 125
Chapman's Ace Hardware 84
Chapman, Sennie 89
Chautauqua 127
Chevrolet 103
Christmas 66, 68, 69, 73, 81, 86, 97, 116–118, 122–124, 126, 128
Church Street 18–20, 112
Cinderella Shoppe 52, 88, 134
City Cafe 26, 43, 91, 108, 109, 111, 118, 125, 128, 131, 143
City Cleaners 72
City Finance 83
City Furniture 20, 91
City Loan 89
Civil War 45
C. K. Carter General Merchandise 65–68, 69, 115, 117, 123, 125, 129, 137, 139, 140
Claussen, Kevin 50
Clayton, Theodore 61, 63
Clingo, Mr. 38
Cobb, Mr. 140
Coffee House 73, 74, 77
Coiffures by Paula 77
Coker, Jimmy 111, 112
Coker, Susie 112
Coleman's Singer Sewing Machines 20
Collins, G. A. 54
Communications (cell phones) 48
Conn, John 105
Corman, Minor 112, 113
cotton 3, 4, 42, 43, 69, 115, 120, 123, 130, 135, 138, 141
Cotton + Company 75

Index

cotton gins 4, 42, 115, 120, 130
Country Charms 76
Country Club 25
Country Junction 57, 71, 89
Cowart, Loutitia 112
Crawford, C. B. 25
Crawford's Cafe 25, 26
Credit Bureau of Escambia County 79
Creek Theatres 29
Crimson Trucking Company 23
Crook, Elise 21, 26, 36, 50, 61, 81, 106
Crook, Fosdick 97, 106
Crook, George C. 104, 140
Crook Hotel 104, 140
Crook, Mattie Lou 22, 26, 28, 43, 106, 109, 110, 112
Crook, Wheeler 109, 131
Cruit, Ada 113, 136
Cruit Office Supply Company 54
Cruit, R. F. 54
Cruit, Robert 106, 141
Cuban Missile Crisis 87
Cunningham and Sons State Farm Insurance 91
Cunningham boys 127
Cunningham, Kimbrell 91
Currie, Barbara 91, 127
Currie, Dan 42
Currie, Hector 126
Currie, H. W. 106, 141
Currie's Gin 42, 69, 115, 130
Curtis-Brooks grocery 65
Curtis, Fred 81
Curtis, Jack 54
Curtis, Jake 91
Curtis Mercantile 57, 61, 62, 104
Custom Travel 94

D

Daniels, Paula 24
Danziger, Helaine. *See* Birnberg, Helaine Danziger
Danziger, Libby 57
Danziger, Mose 57, 96, 116
Danziger's 56–58
Darby, Shirley 90
Dauphin, Ray 78
Davis, Bobby 21, 106
Davis, Chice 85
Davis, Hazel 133
Davis, Mable 107
Davis, Pinkie 119
Davisville, Alabama 119
Dawe, Darryl 71, 78
Day Gallery 27, 28
Day, Joel 19, 51, 59, 64, 66, 78, 88, 89, 94, 100, 103, 104, 108
Day, Louise 19, 51, 64, 94
Dean's Chevron Station 113
Decorating Center 44
Deese, Mayor 127
Dees, H. H. 78, 82, 100
Dees, Hillary Herbert (Hub) 84
dentists 36, 49, 50, 52, 56, 57, 61, 97, 106
depot 95, 104, 107, 129, 131
Designs on Living 57
Dew, Jack and Claytie 26
D&G Finest Cuts 48
Diana Shop 63
Dickinson and Barnett Furniture 21
Dickinson Furniture 21
Dickinson, L. E. 21
Dickson, Hugh 137
Digmon, Sherry 22
Diller, Connie 64
Discount Tax 58
Dixie Blend Coffee 73
Dixie Cafe 103
Dorriety, Greg 23
Dorriety, Gwen 23, 24
Doty, Mrs. 81
Doug's Billiard Parlor 99
Downey, Louie Finch Sharpless 25
Dress For Less 63, 64
Dugout 77
Dunaway, Bill 20, 65, 66, 67, 119, 120
Dunaway, Mildred Carter 64, 65, 66, 67, 102, 119, 120
Dunn, Frances Earle 57, 60, 65
Dunn, Wayne 60
Dunn, Winston 33, 55

E

Earle, Herman 60, 97, 104
Earle, Margarette 26, 49, 52, 56, 59, 61, 88, 90, 100, 104, 108
Earle's Jewelry 58, 59, 60, 125, 129
Easter 119
Eats Shop 58
Economy Shop 38
Economy Store 59, 61
Eddins, Jimmy 119
Edgar, Billy 89, 92
Edgar's 54, 88, 89
Edie's Craft Shop 102
Edward Jones company 44, 49, 51
Edwards Building 111
Edwards, Mr. 109
Eleanor's House of Beauty 20
elections 128, 130
Electric Shoe Shop 98
Elite Barber Shop 50, 130, 134, 137
Elite Sporting Goods 81
Ellis, Cecil 70
Ellison, Linda Lumpkin 118–119
Ellis's grocery 70
Elmore's 5&10 Store 26, 37, 38, 39, 124, 137
Elsie Schott 19
Emmons Hotel 3
Encore at the Strand 28
Episcopal Church 26
Episcopalians 26, 128
Ernest Ward school 26
Escambia County High School 25, 84, 120–121, 127, 128, 136
Escambia County Junior High School 93, 139
Escambia County offices 92, 93
Escambia County Training School 129
Escambia Drug Store 33–36, 55, 61, 69, 108, 124, 127, 133, 134, 136, 142
Escambia Farm Equipment 76
Escambia Hardware 106, 107, 134, 141
Esneul, Hugo 41, 85, 91
Ethridge, Earl 91
Everedge, C. C. 32

F

Factory Connection 38
Faircloth, Mack 100
Faircloth, Rob 41
Faircloth, Roderick 78
Faircloth's Grocery 19, 125
Faircloth, Taylor 61
Fair Department Store 85
Fall Festival 111
Farish, Dr. 60, 89
Farmers' Supply 78
Farmhouse Antiques 57
Farm Security 87
Farm Supply 82
Fayard, Elam 98
Fayard, Sarah 98

Fayard's Jewelers 98, 106
Fehr, Chris and Brandy 50
Financial Solutions 23
fires 27, 41, 53, 59, 66, 99, 102, 103, 113, 126, 127, 137
Firestone Tires 103
First Assembly of God 100
First Baptist Church 57, 79, 126, 127, 128, 136
First Methodist Church 127, 130
First National Bank 3, 35, 48, 79, 80, 97, 98, 106–107, 109, 125, 126, 129
First Presbyterian Church 25
Fischer, Larry 35, 73, 77, 81, 111, 121
Fischer, Lawrence Eugene "Gene", Jr. 74
fish market 70
Flomaton, Alabama 35, 45, 46, 73, 74, 109, 111, 141
Florida Fabrics 82
Floyd, Coach 121
Forget-Me-Not 21
Forte Furniture 75, 76, 78, 82, 85
Forte Furniture Annex 72
Forte Furniture Warehouse 75
Forte, James 21, 22, 26, 28, 31, 32, 36, 38, 40, 41, 42, 44, 49, 51, 59, 60, 61, 63, 64, 66, 70, 76, 81, 82, 84, 86, 89, 91, 92, 99, 100, 101, 103, 110
Forte, Jerrye Sue 128
Forte, Russell 100
Forte's Discount Furniture 63
Foster, Clara Hodnette 59
Frank, Emily Woodson 81
Frazier, Cliff 22, 38, 78, 81, 92, 93, 94, 101, 133
Frazier, Gladys 133
Frazier, Will 81
Frazier, W. L. (Willie) 94
Fred's 37, 38

Fred's Barber Shop 109
French, Ted 81, 113
The Frisco 44, 45
Frisco City, Alabama 46, 74
Fuller, Jim 69
Fuller's Grocery Store 63, 69, 70
Funk, Ethel Grimsley 88
Furney, Arabell Cain 111
Furney, Cleo 111
Furney, G. F. 111
Furney, Lloyd F., Jr. 111
Furney, Lloyd (Sandy), Sr. 111
Furney, Samuel Franklin 111
Furney's Bakery 128

G

Gainus' Blacksmith Shop 69, 140
gambling 137
Gandy, A. L. 52
Gandy Shoe Shop 52, 70
Garrard, John 108, 140
Gather Restaurant 40, 41
Gayle's Income Tax 20
George and Lumpkin Coal Company 107
George, Elizabeth 84
George, Fred 106, 107, 133
Gerlach 103
Gerlach's Main Street Grill 27
Gerlach, Tommy 26, 74
Gidden's Beauty Shop 20
Gilmore Grocery 61
Gladys and Dewey Johnson's clothing store 61
Glam Shak 53
Global Enterprise 61
G. N. Harris old stand 65
Godwin, Willena 26
Goldsmith, Dr. 108

Goldsmith, Earl 84
Goldsmith, Earl and Bertha 113
Goldsmith, E. F. 53, 141
Goldthwaite, Anne 87
Goldthwaite, George 87
Gomilla, Adeline Patterson 38, 52
Gomilla's beauty shop 38
Goodyear store 86, 103
Gordon, Robert 86
Grace Publishing 22
Grace Was in Their Steps 19
Graham, Autrey 88
Graham-Brooks 43–44, 90, 91, 137
Graham Oil Company 103, 137
Graham, Thomas Alexander 43, 103, 104
Gray, Maggie 112
Great Day Discount Store 56
Great Depression 63, 78, 85, 91, 100, 103
Greater Escambia Council for the Arts 42
Greater Fair 21, 66, 84, 99, 124, 133, 140
Green, Beck 51
Greenlawn Pharmacy 33
Greyhound 119
Griffin, Virginia 52, 54, 88
Grimes Cafe 103
Grimes, Elizabeth 113
Grimsley, Bernice 32
Grimsley's Department Store 32, 88, 115, 124, 127, 139
Gross, Stephen 83
G&R Satellite 94
Grubbs' Cafe 103
Grubbs, Hattie 102, 103, 113, 126
Grubbs, Mr. 126
Gulf Winds 113

Gulsby, Voncile 51

H

Haberdashery 99, 101, 102, 103, 104
Hadley, Lorena 91
Hadley's Beauty Shop 91
Hainjie's building 86
Hair Creations 91
Haley, Ben 53
Hall, Charlie 69
Hall, Clayton 78
Hall, Ophelia 91
Hall's Cafe 102
Hall's Income Tax 20
Hall's Tax Services 79
Hammack, Drunetta 24, 89, 91, 92, 100, 103, 112
Hampton House 127
Hand, T. M. 18
Happy Dayz Diner 103
Harper Dry Goods 24
Harper, Haywood 19
Harper, Oscar 25
Harper, Willodean 112
Harvey, John Mason 137
Havard, J. S. 60
Hawke, Hattie Lee 103
Hawt Mess 33
Health Plus Chiropractic Center 83
Healthy Minds Consulting 91
Heat Sports Grill 88, 89
Heavenly Escape Spa 48, 52, 108
Helena Chemical Company 76
Helen's Beauty Shop 134
Helton's 82
Hendrix Tractor 138
Henley's Men's Shoppe 22
Henry Lynch Jewelry Store 90
Heritage Park 4

Hilton, Mr. 90
"History of Atmore, Alabama and Surrounding Area" 73
History of the Bank of Atmore 104
Hobbs, Freddy 85
Hodnette, Mary 116, 127
Hodnette, Robert 116, 130, 136
Hoehn Appliance store 103
Hoehn, John 103
Hoehn, Johnny 38, 85, 86, 103
Hoehn's Trading Center 103, 125
Hoehn's Trading Post 86
Holiday, Annie Ruth 127
Holland, Joe 109
Holley Block 69, 70
Holley, Ruth 69, 113
Holley, W. R. 33, 55, 56, 57, 59, 69, 70, 78, 113, 127
Holmes, George 69
Home Style Furniture 61
Honey's 64
Hopkins, Troy 137
Horne, Frank 56, 60
Horner Street 25, 32, 83
Horn, Son 102
Hotel Carney 104
House of Lowery Tourist Home 113
H&R Block 89, 91
The Humming Bird 45
Hurd, Clint 119
Hurd, Mary Nan 119
Hurricane Erin 105
Hurricane Ivan 19, 27
Hurricane of 1926 100
Hurricane Opal 105
Hurricane Park 35
Hustler's Mercantile 33
Huxford, Alabama 74
Huxford, C. C. 106

I
ice house 83, 119, 131, 135
Infinity Health Care Management 48
International Harvester 84
Irons Five and Dime 63

J
Jack's Barber Shop 20
Jackson, Ernest 61
Jackson, Mr. 59
jail 19, 69, 127
Jasmine Place 56–58, 58
Jay, Alabama 73, 86
Jaycees 52
J&D Discount City 85
Jean Shop 62
Jenkins, Loree 100
Jenkins Superette 100
Jenko, Carolyn Fischer 74
Jernigan, Abner 140
Jernigan, Bea 140
Jernigan, Glenn 119
Jernigan, Mary 119
Jeter, Mr. 86
Jewish 32, 54, 56, 57, 99
Jitney Jungle 61, 63, 125
J&K Variety 64, 124, 142
Joe Albert's Grocery 64
Joey's Furniture 82, 85
John Dixon record hop 144
John's Dry Cleaners 88, 134
Johnson, Dewey 65
Johnson, Gladys 65
Johnson's Dry Goods 65
Jones, Dick 35, 102
Jones Framing 102
Jones, Gloria Marshall 115
Jones, Helen 53
Jones, Johnny 19, 35
Jones, John Paul 85
Jones Motor Company 42, 134
Jones, R. Leon 40, 41, 42
Jones True Value Hardware 77
Joyce's 62, 63
"juke joints" 116
Junky Pearl 62, 70, 78
Jus Because 41

K
K9 Cleaners 72
Karate Studio 40
Karrick, Charles ix, 20, 65, 104
Karrick, Nancy B. ix–xi, 20, 66, 115, 119–124, 139
Kearley store 40
Kearley, Thompson 39
Kelley, Joey 29, 78
Kelley, Wayne and Dawn 29
Kelly, Joey 84, 100
Kelly, Tom 34, 51
Kennington, Albert Spurgeon 124–125, 125
Kennington, Florence Jones 125–127
Kenwin's 64
K&E Pets 70
King Cotton 3
King, John 84
King, Marvin 70, 76
Kizer, June 137
Kizer, Rubye Lee 93
Knoblock's 142

L
Lackey, Mrs. 139
Lambert, Joel 74, 77
Lamont and Sowell Garage 21, 127, 140
Lamont, Willie 21, 127
Lance's Outlet 36
Landrum, Doris 84
La Petite Maison Antiques 91
Lassiter, Ray 38
Latino, Bonnie Bartel 128–129
Laue, Chuck 58
Lazareth, Cy 99
Lazureth, Sam 54
Lee, Ab 102
Lee's David Discount Store 78
Lee's General Merchandise 61
Lee's Music Store 38, 91
Leveret, Mrs. 30
Lewis, Herman 51
Liles Building 90
Liles, E. S. 90
Linda's Hair Fashions 20
Linda's Lane 58
Lions Club 103
Lisenby, J. O. 138
Little Pink Boutique 89
livery stables 65, 69, 115, 136, 137, 140
livestock auctions 138
L&N. See Louisville and Nashville Railroad
Lockwood, Margaret 134
logging 126, 129, 137, 141. See timber
Logie's Bakery and Cafe 27
Lone Wolf graphics 83
Long, Carolyn 127
Long Ford 86
Long, Jimmy 64, 120
Long, Kathryn 64, 120
Long Motor Company 84, 85, 86, 132
Long, Robert "Bob" 40, 52, 85
Looking Glass Beauty Shop 38
Looking Good Gifts and Accessories 64
Louisville and Nashville Railroad 3, 44, 45, 46, 57, 95, 107, 121, 138
Lowery, Florence 29

Lowery, Henry 33
Lowery House 29
Lowery Mercantile 29
Lowery, Rankin 25
Lowery, Root 82
Lowery, Winton W. 29
Lowery, W. W. 3, 24, 25, 29
Lowrey, Charles 25, 26
Lowrey, Nancy 23
Lucas, Ethel 115, 129
Lufkin, Jack 22, 25, 44, 52, 54, 57, 88, 91, 101, 106
Lufkin, Mariott 81
Lufkin, Vera 22, 51
Lumpkin, Helen Ramsey 38, 39, 54, 86, 87, 91, 92, 112, 129–130, 133
Lumpkin, Jim 107
Lumpkin, J. O. 106, 107, 134
Lumpkin's beauty parlor 133
Lumpkin's Pure Gas Station 40
Lumpkin, W. E. "Red" 40
Lundberg, Beverly Bristow 55, 130–133
Luttrell, Betty Kelly 42
Luttrell, Randolph 42
Lynch, Bertha 140
Lynch, Mary 88

M

Magnolia and Company 81
Magnolia Hotel 3, 53
Main Street xi, 5–10, 14, 17, 21–39, 68, 81, 96, 111, 117, 127, 138, 141
Main Street Arcade 38
Main Street Fitness Center 52
Main Street Jewelers 98, 106
Malone, Mr. 24
Manning, E. E. 109
Manning, Mr. 90
Mardi Gras 119

Marie's Ceramics 100
Mark Brown Investment 51
Mark's Barber Shop 92
Martin Automotive Company 84
Martin Auto Park and Chevy 103
Martin Construction 44
Martin, Darcy 66
Martin, R. E. 29
Martin Theaters 29
Mascaro, Kerra 77
Masland Carpet 92
Mason, Bud 91
Mason, Edgar 103
Masonic Hall, Lodge 19, 20, 27
Mason, Jimmy 91
Maxwell Air Force Base 55
Maxwell, Ben 17
Maxwell, Bess Chapman 84
Maxwell, Finklea 55
Maxwell-Haley Building 52, 53, 141
Maxwell, Haley, & Castleberry Insurance 141
Maxwell, Joe 53
Maxwell, Randolph 53, 60, 91, 107
Maxwell, Richard 84
Maxwell, Robert 17, 19, 21, 22, 24, 25, 26, 28, 29, 31, 50, 52, 54, 60, 89, 90
Maxwell, Willie 55
Maxwell, W. R. 52, 53, 141
Maxwell, W. R., Jr. 18
Mayo, W. T. 61, 104
Mays, Edith Cruit 115, 135–136
Mays, Mac 54
McConnico, W. K. 18
McCoy, Bill. *See* Railroad Bill
McCoy Building 42
McCoy, Foster 63
McCoy, J. C. 60
McCoy, J. E. 59, 60

McCoy, L. B. 63, 97
McCoy, Les 42
McCoy, Leslie 69
McCoy, Mr. 103
McCoy, President 104
McCoy's Seed and Feed 70
McCoy, Thera Kelly 27, 31, 42, 63, 81, 97
McCullough, Alabama 46
McDonald, Peanut 38
McElhaney, Chris 27
McGhee, Calvin 67, 68, 140
McGill, Lowell 22, 28, 30, 49, 63, 64, 85, 86, 90, 99, 133
McGill, Ouida 31
McGraw, J. S. 98
McKinley, Ann 133
McKinley, John 86
McKinley, Kevin 20, 91, 134–135
McMillan, Ed 46
McMurphy, Dr. 60
McMurphy, James 97, 106
McNeely, Eddie 119
McNeely, Retha 90, 97, 104
McNeely, Roy B. 104
McNeely's Jewelry 90, 97, 104, 106, 125
Medical Park Drive ii
Memories of Banbury ix
Merle Norman Beauty Center 23
Merriwether feed barn 142
Merriwether, Jake, Sr. 69
Methodists 79, 126
Michelle's Baking Company and Cafe 57
Middleton, Haskew 17, 19, 21, 24, 26, 28, 30, 32, 35, 38, 53, 84, 85, 86, 87, 91, 93, 100, 102, 103, 106, 109, 110, 113
Middleton, Pam 128
Middleton, Zolan 38, 99, 101

milkmen 135
Miller, George 66
Miller, Lillian 88
Mills, James 109, 111
Millson, Dr. 49, 50, 52
Mill Street 135
Mills, Virginia 109, 111
Mims, Dr. 56, 127
Mims, Emilie 71
Mims Stained Glass Studio 71
Mims, Zollie 36, 57, 61
Mini Maids 72
Miracle Ear Hearing Aid Service 101
Monroe, Myrna 22
Monroeville, Alabama 74, 137
Moore, B. C. 84, 85
Moore, Otis 90
Morgan, Grace 109
Morris, Sam 99
Morris, Sye 54
Mosley, Hunter 50
Moulton, Charlie 57
Movie Time Video and Arcade 22
Mrs. D's Tax Service 75
mule barn 84
murals 87
Murray Johnson Insurance 93
Music Express 73
Myer, L. 61, 104

N

Nall, Harry 52
Nall, James 33, 38
Nall, Marshall 103
Nall, Melvin 22
Nall's Family Grocery 124, 133
Nancy's Etc. 94
Nancy's Hair Salon 94, 128
Nan's Main Street Cafe 27

Index

Nashville Avenue 16, 22, 65, 86, 104, 106, 142
National Butane 82
National Guard Armory 144
Native Americans 67, 79, 140
Nelson, Mary 129
Nelson, Mrs. 38
Nelson Place 62
Nettles, Dr. 60
New Dimensions Custom Picture Frames & Gifts 53
New Me Center Beauty Shop 48
News Room 91
New York Fashions 38, 63, 64, 84
New York Life Insurance 23, 58
Nichols and Cobb accounting office 91
Nichols' Department Store 66
Nichols, I. G. 66
Nokomis, Alabama 124
No Returns 63
Norman Hotel 104, 141
Norman, M. R. 104
Norman, Theodosia 104
Norris, Edgar 31, 36, 38, 40, 53, 63, 66, 74, 78, 85, 91, 92, 100, 101, 103, 106, 110
North Carolina 80
Northrup Grocery 110, 112
Northrup, Henderson 110
Northrup Seed 92
Northrup, Voncile 110

O

Odom, Ralph 71
OK Barber Shop 20, 97, 125
Olan Mills 104
Olen's 63
O'Neal, Bill 134
optometrists 83, 89

Oriental Trading 61
Otis Moore Law Firm 90
Otis Wise Insurance 49
Owens, Rodney 83

P

Parish Grill 27
Parker, Curtis 136–138
parks 17, 35, 98, 100, 109, 119
Parmer, Brannon 83
PCI Printing 82
Peacock, Claude 77
Peacock Photography 91
Peacock's Atmore Barber Shop 77
Peacock's Barber Shop 136, 143
Peacock's poolroom 136
Peacock Stationery and Storage 91
Peavy, Dee 54
Peavy, Jane 18, 20
Peavy, Julian F. 49, 51, 52, 54, 60, 79, 80, 97, 106, 108, 134, 138
Peavy, Mary 54
Peavy, Mrs. J. T. 52
Peavy-Webb Building 79
Pensacola Avenue 69, 106, 107, 108, 113, 124, 125, 126, 135, 139
Pensacola, Florida 4, 23, 46, 96, 118, 120, 122
People's Mercantile Company 61
Pepperman, Marcia Webb 19, 51, 80, 108, 138–139
Pepsi-Cola Bottling Company 107
Pfeifer Bakery 86
Philanthropic Seed 75
Phillips Specialty Store 31
Piggly Wiggly 110, 112, 133
Pinto, Jose 27
Pintoli's 27
Pipkin, E. L. 3

Pipkin, James and Zema 26
Pittman, Cleveland and Katie 113
Polk's Directory 24, 56, 61, 71, 72, 97, 98, 99, 100, 102
Pollard, Alabama 45, 61, 104
Ponder, Dr. 52
pool halls 97, 98, 99, 102, 125, 137, 143
post office 91, 104
Powell, Carey 25
Premier Glass 44
Presley, Bernece 23
Pressley Street 73
Publican 77
Pullen Metal Supply 75
Pullen's TV Repairs 75
Pure Oil Company 40

Q

Quarker, Anna Bell 115, 139–140

R

Rabon, Mary Carter 64, 65, 96, 117
Rachel Patterson school 118
Rackard, Ruthie Mae 115, 140
Radio Shack 33
Ragan, David 102
Ragan framing 102
Railroad Bill 3, 46
railroads 3, 4, 42, 45–46, 92, 95–96, 104, 126, 129, 130
Rains Insurance 53
Ralph's Barber Shop 71, 72
Ramsey, Hugh 86
Randal's 61
Randolph Maxwell and Bob Long car loans 91
Rankin, Mrs. 102
Ray's Barber Shop 130

Reconstruction 87
Red Cross 94
Reflections: Conversations with Some of Atmore's Senior Citizens 115
Regina's Unlimited 75
Reid Barber Shop 110
Reid Drug Store 34, 50, 51, 115, 125, 128, 132, 134, 142, 143
Reid, J. A. 51
Reid's barber shop 51
religion 26, 51, 75, 79, 91, 100, 115, 119, 126, 143
Rent-to-Own 101
Repton, Alabama 65, 74
Rex Sporting Goods 50, 52, 125, 128, 130
Reynolds, Lisa 72
Reynolds' Real Estate 72
Rhodes, Grady 61
Ridgeley Street 12–13, 67, 69, 137
Ringling Brothers Circus 96
Rising Stars Studio of Dance 76
Risque Boutique 48
R&J Wholesale Florist 76
Roaster's Gallery 73
Roberts family 108
Roberts' store 3
Robinson Butane 82
Robinson's gin 115
Robinsonville, Alabama 134, 141
Rodgers, H. H., Sr. 49
Rollins, S. L. 28, 140
Rollo, Helen 26
Rollo, Tom 26
Roosevelt, Franklin D. 87
Rosser, Mr. 89
"round-a-bout" 137
Rowlands Tire Center 103
Royal Dollar Store 56

Rozelle, Hugh 60
Ruffles Butane 92

S

Salley, George 104
Sam's Place 103
Sawdust Box 102
sawmill 3, 45, 80, 126, 129, 141
Scoggin, George 99
Seale, Lee Verne 107
Securance Insurance group 53
Selective Service 87
Selma, Alabama 57
Serenity Heart Home Health Care 49, 91
S&G Collectibles 77
Shackleford, Dr. 83
Shane Cooper attorney's office 48
Shanks, Charlie 36
Sharpless, Carlton 111
Sharpless, Collie 25
Sharpless Furniture 64, 69, 82
Sharpless, Guy 25, 51
Sharpless, Johnny 25, 44
Sharpless, Louie 25
Sharpless, Martha 25, 44
Sharpless, Mrs. 131
Sharpless, O. H. 78, 100
Sharpless, Roy 25
Sharpless' Sweet Shop 109
Sharpless, Virginia 44
Sharpless, Will 25
Shaver, Lewis 109, 110, 112
Shell, Howard 140–141
Shirley Darby's Law Office 90
Shiver, John 44, 82, 83, 87, 94, 99, 102
Shoe Hospital 125
Shopper's Bazaar 40
Sider's Shoe Repair 71

silk mill 103
Simmons, Dennis 41
Simply Agnes 22
Simpson's Grocery 61, 63, 64
Singer shop 81
Sisters 52
Skinner's Jewelry 73
Skipper Insurance Company 23
Skipper-Phillips Insurance Agency 97
Slater, Morris. *See* Railroad Bill
Sleep Shop 77
Sleepy Hollow Water Beds and Furniture 61
Smith, Agnes 21, 99, 124, 133
Smith, Elizabeth 127
Smith, Francis Drew 88
Smith, Gail 28, 40, 110, 133
Smith, Henley 22, 124
Smith, Mrs. Paul 54
Smith, Nick 94
Smith, Ruby 110
Smith's Bakery 111
Smith Trading Company 28
Snyder, Earl 112
Snyder-White Furniture 111, 112, 125
soda fountains 33, 34, 35, 36, 51, 84, 118, 128, 131, 142
Solomon, Frances 21
Southern Addictions—Antiques and Consignment 62
Southern Charms and More 57
Southern Computer 91
Southern Gold Buyers 91
Southern Link 48
Southern Social Boutique 78
Southern Stems 59
Southland Telephone 113
Sowell, Catherine 21
Sowell, Charlie 21, 127

Sowell, Margaret 21, 84
Stabler, J. W. 60
Stabler's Shoe Repair 98
Staff, Ann Hoehn 101, 103
Stallworth, Burton 76
Stallworth, Jack 138
Stallworth's Clothing Store 133
Stallworth, Tommy 38, 39, 56, 60
Stanley, Leonard 19
Stanton, Commander 19
State Farm Insurance 89
State Line Pawn Shop 91
State Line Tax 58
State Line Tires 103
state prison farm 57
Steele, Charlie 22, 112
Steele, Claude 112
Steele, Ebo 98
Steele, Ernest "Big Steele" 44
Steele's Cash and Carry 22, 26
Steele's Curb Market 125
Stewart, Abbie 48, 51, 108, 138
Stewart, Ava 108, 129, 138
Stewart, Grandma 111
Stewart House 107, 125, 138
Stewart, Jack 108
Stewart, James 46
Stewart, John 91, 137
Stewart's Pool Room 136
Stilling, Russell 99
Still, Merrill 110, 111, 112
Stokes, Clyde 37
Stone, E. S. 28
Strand Theatre 3, 29–31, 113, 124, 128, 133, 134, 139, 142
street musicians 143
Stuart, Little John Harvey 99
Stuart's Billiard Parlor 99
Style Shop 53, 54, 88

Sunny Skies 63
Superdome 35
Superior Family Support Services 91
Sutton, Doc 74, 103
Sutton's Music 73
Sutton's Restaurant 103
Sweet Shop 25, 91, 109, 128, 133, 142, 143
Sweet Shop Cafe 124
Swift, Byard 19, 22, 36, 38, 39, 40, 41, 49, 51, 61, 81, 84, 86, 92, 99, 103
Swift, G. R. 106, 107
Swift, J. B., Sr. 18
Swift, Lucille King 88
Swift, Margarita 84

T

taxi 115
Tax Prep Evolution 92
Taylor Faircloth's fabric store 20
Taylor, Norma 64
Taylor, Pappy 20
Taylor, Peyton 109
Taylor, Ruth 53
Taylor's Barber Shop 20
Teate's Grocery 64
telegraph office 79
Temple, J. C. 88
Temple, Mrs. J. C. 53, 88
Tennant, Alton 35, 137
Tennant, Lottie 75
Tennant's Cafe 75, 137
Tennant's Meat Market 70, 71
Tensaw River 3, 45
Texas 74, 79, 115
Thames, Otis 39
Thanksgiving 120, 122, 123, 124
"The Letter Box" 87
30 Below 88, 89

Index

Thomas, James 49
Thomas, Nell 38, 49, 53, 59, 63, 66, 71, 72, 101, 103
Thomas the Pig 71
Thomasville, Alabama 104
Thompson, Clarence 88
Thompson's Fine Fashions 99
Thompson's Home Furnishings 83
Thornbloom, Cecil 48
Threadgill, Patricia Crook 36
Tidmore and Ward's 3, 46
Tiger Lily 50
timber 3, 45, 87, 92, 135
Tims, Byron 38
Tiny Diner 142
T. J.'s Hair Repair Beauty Shop 48
Tot Shop 23, 52, 101, 133
Trace Patrick Apparel 50
Tradin' Post 70, 78, 100
Trammell Street 61, 69, 90
Transport Trucking 91
Treherne, Ann 89
Treherne, Dr. 49
Treherne, Mrs. 89
Tremmer, Mrs. 108
Trimmer, A. T. 101
Trimmer, Bernard 103
Trimmerz Hair and Nails 92
Turner, Clint 115, 141
turpentine 3, 45, 135
TV and Recap 103

U

U Financial 81
United Bank 39, 40, 66, 104–105
Uriah, Alabama 74, 88, 139
USDA Farmers Home Administration 97
U.S. Navy Recruiting Station 20

V

Valentine's 132
Varner, Bill 138
Vaught Hospital 129
Vickery, Sheryl 46
Vickrey, Red 103
Vickrey, Weldon 35
Vic's 38
Vin-Tiques 71
VW Finance 92

W

Wade, Brenda 52
W. A. Grimsley and Son 31
Wainwright Construction 104
Wallace Store 64
Waller, Hal 97, 106
Walnut Hill 25, 26
Ward, Bill 19
Ward, Murphy 126
Ware, Charlie 141–144
Washington County 79
Washington, Martha 86
Washington Pie 86
washwomen 115
watermelons 35, 36, 137
WATM 26, 53
Watson, Billy 92
Watson Hardware 82, 84, 125, 144
Watson, Rupert 70, 82, 84, 92
Watson's Farmall Tractors 70
Wearren, James 17, 28
Webb, A. P. 28, 59, 60
Webb, Doug 56, 60
Webb, Dr. 79
Webb Home 80
Webb House 79
Webb, Ida 80
Webb, John 19, 21, 41, 43, 49, 51, 53, 55, 56, 63, 64, 66, 69, 79, 80, 81, 85, 88, 90, 91, 100, 102, 103, 108, 109, 111, 112
Webb, Letha (Mrs. Pellar) 28, 120, 139
Webb, Lizzie Lee 79
Webb, Marvin 127
Webb, Pellar 17, 28, 43, 120, 138
Webb Sr., Mrs. A. P. 129
Webb, Tom 138
Weber, Martin 91
We Care 37, 40
Weeks grocery 61
Weeks, Louie 61
Wells, Q. E. 69
West Brothers Clothing 85
Western Auto 27, 28, 40, 109, 110, 125, 133, 134
Western Union 110
Whistle Stop Grill 63
White, A. G. 109
White Furniture 112
White, Tommy 112
Whittaker, Brent 22
Whitten, Annie Ruth 50, 52, 61, 89
Will Hudson's clothing store 53
Williams, H. C. 26, 52, 81, 87, 112, 120
Williams, Nancy 39
Williamson, H. B. 91
Williams, Pearl 120, 139
Williams Realty 41
Williams' Station 3, 45, 141
Williams' Station Cemetery 4
Williams, William Larkin 3, 45
Wilson Avenue 138
Wilson, James 52
Wilson's bookstore 52
Wingard, Mary 22
Wingard's Jewelry 71, 112
Wingard's on Main 22
Wise Insurance 23
Wise, Mr. 41
Wise, Nell 38
Wise, William Henry "Willie" 46
Wisteria 60, 61
WOCO Pep gas station 40
Wolf, Houston 137
Woodson, Claude 81
Woodson's Furniture 75, 81
Woods, Robert 74
Word of God Bookstore 100
Works Progress Administration 87
World War I 18, 52, 55
World War II 18, 19, 34, 41, 53, 73, 85, 115
Wrangler Grill and Steak House 26
W. R. Holley Memorial Library 94
W. R. Maxwell & Sons 52
W. S. Neal school 54

Y

Yancey, William Hugo 73
Yellow Front Store 70, 78, 79
You're My Star Unique Boutique 89
Your Little Pink Boutique 57, 61

Z

Zelm, Bill 35
Zieback & Webb Timber Company 91
Zwefield, Ray 89

1–Looking south on Main Street, around 1910. 2–Looking north on Main Street, after the Model T had come to town. 3–Farm trucks lined up at Currie's Gin. 4–Atmore Hardware in the early days. 5–Carney Mill Company with Dr. Peavy's office and house in the background. 6–Southwest Main Street before paving. 7–Early trains on both the Frisco trestle and L&N tracks.

www.ingramcontent.com/pod-product-compliance
Lightning Source LLC
Chambersburg PA
CBHW050849010526
44107CB00018BA/1229